Pope and the
Context of
Controversy

Douglas
H.
White

Pope and the The Manipulation
Context of of Ideas in
Controversy *An Essay on Man*

The University Chicago
of Chicago Press and London

To the memory of
my mother and father

Iva Roberts White
John Nelson White

International Standard Book Number: 0–226–89494–0
Library of Congress Catalog Card Number: 70–120009
The University of Chicago Press, Chicago 60637
The University of Chicago Press, Ltd., London

Contents

Preface   vii

1   Aims and Methods   1

2   The Best of Possible Worlds   19

3   God as the Soul of the World   41

4   The Place of Reason   74

5   The Vindication of the Passions   126

6   The Ruling Passion   144

7   Self-love as the Motivation to Action   173

Conclusion   192

Index   195

88433

Preface

Since the first chapter of this volume deals with aims and purposes, there is little left for a preface but acknowledgments of the author's gratitude. Also, two procedures might be commented on by way of warning. The first is of some importance. Although I have quoted many lines from *An Essay on Man* within the text of the study itself, I nevertheless assume that the reader will have a considerable familiarity with the entire poem. The existence of these chapters testifies to their author's belief that Pope's poem is worth reading. This study can in no way be substituted for the poem but is entirely supplementary to the reader's experience of the poem itself.

The second procedure is more trivial. I have made no use of the abbreviation *sic*. I am sure that the readers of this volume are aware that eighteenth century practices in matters of spelling, punctuation, capitalization, and italicization were different from those of the twentieth century, and I have attempted to reproduce quotations in their original form. The errors that are to be found (and of course I hope there are none) are there because they remain undetected.

It is a pleasant task to acknowledge the debts I have contracted over the several years in which I have been at work on the subject of this study. I am indebted to all of the editors and annotators of the *Essay on Man* for providing me with the materials basic for beginning a study of the sort that I have attempted. Most especially I should express gratitude to the latest of these scholars, Maynard Mack. I have profited greatly from both his Twickenham edition of the poem and from his unpublished dissertation on the background of the poem. His bibliography, especially, was truly invaluable to me.

I am grateful to the National Endowment for the Humanities for a fellowship that supported me through a summer and a semester while I devoted full time to my investigations. I received valuable assistance from the staffs of Harper Library at the University of Chicago, the Newberry Library, and the British Museum. I received thoughtful and helpful suggestions from two of my colleagues at Loyola University of Chicago, Eileen Baldeshwiler and David Spencer. The administration of Loyola supplied me with assistance in the form of secretarial aid and xeroxing. In its original form as a doctoral dissertation at the University of Chicago, the manuscript profited from the sensitive and watchful eye of Gwin Kolb.

Edward W. Rosenheim, Jr., has been greatly generous of his time and patience. He made many suggestions that were extremely helpful to me, and I hope that I have been able to pass their substance on to my readers. Mr. Rosenheim's personal kindness and his enthusiasm are deeply appreciated.

There is no possibility of adequately acknowledging my debt to Arthur Friedman lest I should make him responsible for faults that are mine alone. It was he who helped me to see the task I undertook, and it was he who supplied me with insightful and creative guidance as I worked my way through it. In later stages, when the original dissertation was being changed into its present form, his continued friendship and encouragement were of value too great for me ever to repay. It is, therefore, a pleasure to acknowledge my debt publicly.

For the labors of my wife, Sarah, on all levels of the production of this book I express my abiding gratitude.

1

Aims and Methods

In the following chapters I have taken a group of inter-related ideas from Alexander Pope's *An Essay on Man* and have submitted them to a kind of scrutiny that is more closely related to intellectual history than to explication of texts or to poetics. I do hope, nevertheless, to make the workings of the poem some-what more apparent as a result of my efforts. I am attempting to clarify some issues that arose in the phil-osophical and theological controversies of the early eighteenth century. Then I intend to relate Pope's ma-nipulation of these same ideas and issues to a spectrum of

thought made up of the varying interpretations controversial-
ists of his time put upon those ideas. It is my hope that, by
comparing Pope's manipulation of ideas with relevant manipulations of his contemporaries, the workings of Pope's mind
will become more precisely comprehensible to those students
whom he continues to fascinate after the lapse of over two hundred years.

I must make it clear from the outset, however, that I have
made no attempt to determine the sources of Pope's ideas, if by
sources one means the works from which he actually acquired
them. I have also preferred to believe that I have not been constructing what would usually be called the "background" of
Pope's poem. The *Essay on Man* presents special problems in
this regard. The proper concern of background studies is with
patterns of ideas similar to those in the primary source. I have
been interested in similarities, but I have also examined those
peculiar clusters of ideas in the *Essay* that ask of the reader a
familiarity with a whole range of variations on specific ideas,
including the assumptions upon which the ideas are based, the
conclusions to which they lead, and the opposing ideas that
they are intended to refute or replace. My researches have con-
vinced me that Pope's poem is involved in urgent controversy.
I have, therefore, attempted to determine what precise lines of
argument various controversies took. In order to determine
this, I have attempted to discover where the issues lay upon
which the argumentative structure of certain substantial, controversial works was founded. My emphasis, therefore, is on
the manipulation of specific arguments rather than on a milieu
of dominant ideas or influential writers.

Since Pope wrote on several subjects that his contemporaries
held to be sufficiently vital to warrant whole volumes of assertion and rebuttal, we in the twentieth century can profit from
knowing what the bases of disagreement were and what range
of reactions certain key ideas elicited. In the following pages
I have attempted to show that there was, indeed, a range of
reaction to several important ideas which Pope used. In order

to do this, I have quoted a variety of other writers on the same subjects. In addition I have tried to fit Pope into the range, or spectrum, of reaction to the ideas under examination by showing both how his ideas are similar to those of other writers and how Pope differs from those writers. This approach stresses what all toilers in eighteenth century literature know. The period was one of vital diversity of opinion, and anyone who attempts to determine what the "age" thought must examine a wide range of ideas rather than select, triumphant assertions.

The poem itself suggests that the reader should know more than one side of most of its arguments. *An Essay on Man* is not a gratuitous piece of system-making but a refutation of specific points of view, specific ideas. Pope included to some extent both the ideas that he rejected and those he submitted in their place. His own comment on his purpose suggests, even further, that he was purposely placing himself within a range of ideas, since he asserts that he was "steering betwixt extremes of doctrine seemingly opposite."[1] If he was consciously steering between extremes, he was referring to a range of ideas rather than to a single refutable position. The range would presumably have limits of relevance; that is, every author's ideas on a subject would not be relevant. Some assertions might be too wild in direction or too radical in implication; but even those authors who worked within the bounds of a similar frame of reference and an acknowledged awareness of supposed orthodoxy (even without agreement on its contents) used many important ideas with a variety of intention that sets up an observable spectrum of implications and interpretations.

If the ideas Pope steered between are *seemingly* opposite, then he evidently felt that they were not necessarily opposite but that some mistake in either the statement of the doctrines or some false conclusion stemming from them made them ap-

1. Alexander Pope, *An Essay on Man,* ed. Maynard Mack (New Haven, Conn.), p. 7. All quotations from the *Essay on Man* will be identified by epistle and line number and will be taken from this edition of the work, hereafter cited as Mack.

pear to conflict. When the implications of an idea are the source of heterodoxy or orthodoxy, then the spectrum of thought formed by a variety of implications becomes important. It is with this spectrum of interpretation and reaction that the following chapters are concerned. The major task is to place Pope accurately in the spectrum.

Ever since the poem's first publication readers have been more inclined to notice that Pope's ideas were commonplace than to perceive them as adjustments and adaptations of widely accepted notions. I have not attempted to demonstrate that his ideas were highly original. At any rate, the observation that an idea is commonplace or that one has heard it before is no indication of the capacity of the idea to engage the interest or the antipathy of large numbers of readers. When one labels and thus dismisses an idea as a commonplace, it may be that he is bored with it or antagonistic toward it—or he may misunderstand it. I will show that at least some of Pope's key ideas were highly controversial, and the willingness of Pope's contemporaries to argue over these ideas suggests to me that they had some urgency both to the people who wrote the books and the people who read them.

It is not always with whole books, however, that one is concerned. Seldom is a whole controversial work aimed at the specific source of difference between the writer and his supposed or real antagonists. In most of the pamphlets described in the following chapters the largest number of pages were spent asserting ideas which neither side doubted. There was usually a crucial point of difference between the disputants, however, and that core of conflict is what stands in greatest need of isolation and examination. There was, for example, small difference between what one writer and another considered to be the content of the moral laws. What men ought to do or ought not to do to their fellow men was seldom at issue.

How they could be made to do what it was agreed they should do was, however, a more complicated problem. The *source* of moral obligation, as this subject of speculation was called, was controversial; on that issue disputants divided into at least two clear schools and several sects within the schools. One school insisted that a virtuous man must abide by the moral laws because the laws are good and because he abstractly loves the beauty and goodness of the laws themselves. The opposing school denied that abstract devotion could play any effective role in the matter since men are motivated by self-love rather than abstract beauty. According to writers of this school men could be made virtuous only by making virtue answer the needs of self-love. The threat of hell would motivate them to avoid it.

In the treatises written by members of both of these schools, however, a great deal of space was frequently devoted to tangential concerns which had nothing to do with the actual issue over the source of moral obligation, and from those passages one would have no way of telling which school the author belonged to, for what he said was very likely not controversial at all. The author's school would be determined by his resolution of the issue (the source of moral obligation), and even a noncontroversial part of his treatise could easily be affected by his stand on the key issue, for saying the right thing for the wrong reason was nearly as bad as saying the wrong thing. Quite harmless or even laudable ideas could become sinister if their author belonged to the wrong school.

It is my hope that my method of handling material relevant to the ideas in *An Essay on Man* will aid the student in perceiving the broad range of thought available to Pope's consideration and will dissuade the student from settling for oversimplified generalizations about either the poet or his period. I also hope to make the working of Pope's mind somewhat clearer by relating it to a contemporary setting. For some purposes at least, Pope's ideas should be compared with those of other writers who lived at the same time and were subject to similar influences. That is to say, his readers should have some sort of realistic standard by which to determine what he can justifiably be held accountable for.

One way to begin to construct such a standard is to show what other writers thought about the same or similar ideas and what range of reactions to those ideas they put into print. My primary concern is with this latter question. I have attempted to determine what I have called the *status* of certain of Pope's ideas. The status of an idea is determined by: (1) its vogue, that is, its appearance in some works of the period with a pretense to timeliness and substance; (2) the reactions to the idea to be found in the works of contemporary writers, including the assumptions on which the idea was thought to be based and the consequences that were thought to result from it. Both parts of the status of key ideas in the *Essay* will be demonstrated in the following pages by an appeal to specific texts rather than to supposed prevalent notions.

At this point, however, one should specify both the most interesting and the most difficult part of the endeavor. There is the uncomfortable feeling that such a process may be based on the curious notion that ideas are stable even though the contexts in which they are to be found may vary, but experience insists that when an idea is put into a noticeably different context, it adjusts itself in such a way as to cease to be the same idea. Two assertions, similar in appearance, that are formed from opposing premises and result in opposing conclusions cannot be the same idea, despite the apparent similarity. The following chapters serve to underline the fact that many of Pope's most important aphorisms are highly ambiguous until they are related to their context. Then a comparison with other contexts demonstrates the multiplicity of reactions and the complexity of argument with which Pope's contemporaries associated those ideas. I have attempted to determine the status of some of Pope's ideas and to see how he used them, not as separable from a context but with the variety of associations they held for Pope's contemporaries. Then I have attempted to show how Pope fits into the contemporary spectrum involving those ideas.

I have examined in this manner a core of ideas that make up

what I conceive to be Pope's most basic assertions about God and man. The parallel lines of reasoning by which he reaches some of his conclusions about both God and man will be noted as they arise. The parallelism is of interest because there was some contemporary doubt that anything about God and man could be accounted for by the same reasoning process. In the parallelism itself, therefore, Pope is committing himself to the controversial position that a single dialectical method will lead men to truths about both God and his creatures.

Throughout Pope's argument the individual assertions are shown for the most part to be commonplace (as we have often been told); but as the commonplaces are examined in a range of contexts, these show that as used by various authors the commonplaces take on different substance, different meanings. The details of the differences are included in the chapters of this study. Pope's relationship to the scale of differences is the subject of the entire inquiry.

An example will give some substance to these general remarks. Though countless authors asserted that infinite wisdom must form the best of possible worlds, the idea was controversial; it elicited controversy not because any writer relevant to Pope's argument wanted to deny the excellence of God's creation but because God's freedom of willing appeared to be threatened by what he *must* do, and God's responsibility for the origin of evil seemed to be implied since, if he must create the best world, everything exists as it does because God created it according to his own specifications. It is quite unlikely that Pope was unaware of these implications of his assertion that infinite wisdom must form the best world, for in Pope's system God's wisdom as a predominant attribute is clearly intended to supersede will as an attribute abstracted from perceptions of value; and thus Pope grants, at least by implication, a limitation on God's will but compensates with what is to him the superior principle of controlling wisdom. That is, Pope's decision, contrary to much contemporary opinion, was that it is more important that God should be subject to the rule of his own wisdom than that he should be free, even though the creation might seem, as a consequence, to be inevitably what it is and God might seem to be directly responsible for the evils of the system recommended to him by his wisdom. Pope mitigates God's responsibility for the origin of evil by making God's relationship to the world analogous to the relationship of a man's soul to his body. Pope then attributes the active functioning of the physical world to a "plastic nature" which supposedly operates in the same way the vegetable soul of man operates as it keeps the processes of growth and healing at work.

One of Pope's concerns in the writing of the *Essay* was to state his case but to extricate himself from certain difficulties perceived by his contemporaries to be attached to the position he favored. He did not choose merely to assert but also to deal with contemporary reaction to the supposed direction of his assertions. One part of my intention in the present study is to discover how well Pope understood the direction of his own argument as it would have been understood by his well-informed contemporaries. I do not, however, intend to decide whether he escaped satisfactorily according to the armed vision of the twentieth century, or even according to the individual conclusions of his contemporaries. Nor would one be justified in asking whether he arrived at the one acceptable adjustment of ideas, for it is perfectly apparent that there neither was nor is any such thing. Some progress can be made, however, toward ascertaining the status and direction of the solutions he employed, which in turn will show us some of the ways in which his mind worked—and, it must be repeated, show this against a contemporary spectrum of opinion rather than against a single set of beliefs, whether of Pope's day or our own.

It has already been mentioned that one example of Pope's manipulative method is to be found in the parallel pattern of argumentation he uses to substantiate his arguments about man and God. As God's dominant attribute is wisdom, man's is passion. God, therefore, is motivated by abstract excellence, but man is motivated by the relationship of objects and actions to his self-love. In the first case the motivation is "right" because God creates, and thus wisdom recommends what will be created; it is right in the second case because man reacts, so it is necessary that he should be placed in a system where his reactions will be appropriate to the elements he encounters. Therefore, a world where "self-love and social are the same" presents no conflict with excellence, even to a creature who is predominantly motivated by self-love.

Pope carries the parallel even further by granting that men have a ruling passion that is, in fact, necessary to produce the variety of motivations required to accomplish the world's work. Here, too, the apparent danger is mitigated by an even stronger and universal motivation—happiness. Again, the general plan is not threatened by self-directed individual men since, by nature, they pursue the common goal of happiness which the system controls to the general benefit.

Because Pope handles not merely inflexible commonplaces but the implications and consequences of his key assertions, he is able to maintain in *An Essay on Man* a tone of well-informed urbanity and also accomplish what I conceive to be the most important example of his steering between extremes of doctrine. This introductory chapter is not the place to supply details, but each of the discussions of single ideas that follows shows that his manipulations are rather wittily carried on by granting to extreme arguments their premises while denying their conclusions or by granting their conclusions though denying their premises. This element of wit has seldom if ever been emphasized in commentaries on the *Essay*, though one supposes that it was sufficiently evident to Pope's contemporaries to require no great notice. Were the arguments obscure or unusual one could not assume that large numbers of readers would react to them with sufficient familiarity to notice rather slight variations or mutations, but in fact many of Pope's most important ideas were widely known and frequently discussed.

The fluid, cajoling, and frequently almost chatty tone of the poem suggests that the context itself ought to have somewhat of a lilt, but the lugubriousness of the surface subject matter may hide the witty, bantering element of the poem from a twentieth-century audience. We have not been constantly bombarded with pamphlets (sometimes going through three editions in a year) attempting once again to settle the question of the foundation of morality and consequently of religious obedience, plus the motivation of God vis-à-vis free will and the origin of evil. That Pope himself may have thought that he was playing with ideas rather wittily is suggested by a report from his friend Joseph Spence, who quotes him as follows:

As L'Esprit, La Rochefoucauld, and that sort of people prove that all virtues are disguised vices, I would engage to prove all vices to be disguised virtues. Neither, indeed, is true, but this would be a more agreeable subject, and would overturn their whole scheme.[2]

It is the "Neither, indeed, is true, but . . ." which I find of particular interest. It suggests that Pope, at least at some times during his life, was more interested in the effect which could be derived by manipulating or refuting well-known points of view than he was with the abstract truth of the system he constructed. This method of playing with ideas from a controversial context seems closer to Pope's own statement that he was trying to put morality in good humor,[3] and it is certainly closer to what we might expect of him from his most original and characteristic works.

Even if Pope's contemporaries did not notice the wit of the *Essay,* it is there. On the other hand, what everyone has noticed is the danger that the whole argument runs of sacrilege. There is, first of all, the treatment of sacred matters in a flippant

2. Joseph Spence, *Observations, and Characters, of Books and Men,* ed. James M. Osborn, 2 vols. (Oxford, 1966), 1:219. This edition quotes manuscript readings that show at least some interest on Pope's part in refuting La Rochefoucauld. Pope's correspondence with Swift on the subject can be found in George Sherburn, ed., *The Correspondence of Alexander Pope,* 5 vols. (Oxford, 1956), hereafter cited as Sherburn.
3. Sherburn, 3:117.

manner; Pope is frequently too light and sprightly for the pious. Then there is the avoidance of reference to specific doctrines of Christianity. Here the student must not forget that the first half of the eighteenth century delighted in a game long since fallen out of fashion. A system of natural religion was the result of an author's attempt to construct a moral and/or theological system by reason alone. When a writer set out to construct a system of natural religion, he no more denied the efficacy of the Christian revelation than a man who sets out to lift a weight with his right arm denies the existence of his left. Such a writer was merely setting a task for himself with acknowledged limitations.

Pope's *Essay* is a system of natural religion (other examples would be William Wollaston's *The Religion of Nature Delineated* and Archbishop William King's *Essay on the Origin of Evil,* as well as several of the lectures subsidized by the bequest of Robert Boyle for the purpose of confuting atheism). If Pope was to be true to the game he was playing, the Christian revelation was ruled out of the discussion. Such systems were intended, in the hands of the orthodox, to make use of reason alone to demonstrate the validity of religious doctrines that had been questioned, presumably on the grounds of reason alone. Usually the systems were intended to demonstrate that Christian conclusions were attainable through reasonable processes, but often there was a point at which revealed doctrine was found necessary lest the writer should find himself engulfed in downright deism.[4] (The immortality of the soul was frequently the point at which revelation became indispensable.)

4. R. S. Crane gives a workable definition of deism: ". . . the essence of deism, it was now more than ever clear, lay in its radical assertion, against Christianity, of the principle that any religion necessary for salvation must be one that has always and everywhere been known to men" (" Anglican Apologetics and the Idea of Progress, 1699–1745," *Modern Philology* 31 [1934]:282). In order to show the relationship of deism to natural religion, I define a deist as one who espouses the *sufficiency* of natural religion. An Anglican, therefore, who defended the *excellence* of natural religion but did not hold it to be sufficient for man's moral needs would not be a deist. See note 10 below.

The popularity of the game did not, however, guarantee acceptance by contemporaries, and the danger of exclusive reliance on reason unaided by revelation was evident to nearly everybody. Actual deists, such as Matthew Tindal, took evident pleasure in quoting the great natural religionist and archbishop of Canterbury, John Tillotson in their defense. Nevertheless, although many writers feared that the Christian revelation would cease to appear necessary in a system where reason alone was called to testify, and although the touchy reacted nervously to such attempts as (at least) latent deism, the game was widely enjoyed and widely understood. Even when Christian divines demonstrated the reasonableness of Christianity most seriously there was probably an element of wit in defeating the deists with their own weapons.

The important point is that, for many writers contemporary with Pope, the absence of specific Christian reference from their religious treatises was no indication that Christian doctrines were in doubt, but only that these writers were abiding by the rules of the game. Pope's handling of his material could have been intended to show that arguments from reason reach the same conclusions as those from Christian doctrine. He shared with many overtly Christian writers the basic belief that man is a creature motivated by passion rather than reason, who stands in need of assistance from authority. Still, except perhaps where Pope looked longingly at immortality, he wrote largely within his self-imposed limits.[5]

Having noticed that systems of natural religion were usually intended to convince atheists, or perhaps deists, of the reasonableness of Christianity, one should also notice that the supposed adversary of Pope's poem is probably neither of these. Though certain passages in Pope's argument have suggested to some of his readers that he assumed what he was responsible for proving, a more charitable conclusion might be that his

5. Actually, even here Pope stays within the imposed limits. The early deists at least accepted immortality as being available to reason, and Pope proves it with a syllogism.

adversary, not he, accepted certain conclusions too easily. On the other hand, when, in the poem, Pope is asserting rather than refuting, his argument is usually directed only to someone who grants what he takes for granted.

There is, to be sure, something a trifle ingenuous in the frequently encountered process of determining an author's intended audience by showing who would find his argument appealing. Nevertheless, from at least two of Pope's specific references to methods of argumentation we must conclude either that he did not know what he ought to have been doing or that his antagonist (at least at those moments) was someone who accepted certain propositions and should have accepted others which, according to Pope, ought to follow from them. I, at least, am inclined to give Pope the benefit of the doubt. The objection is far too obvious for him to have missed it.

> Of Systems possible, if 'tis confest
> That Wisdom infinite must form the best,
> Where all must full or not coherent be,
> And all that rises, rise in due degree. . . .
>
> (I, 43–46)

A great deal is "confest" in these lines, but it is evident that Pope regards the propositions as a priori truths.

Rarely in the first three decades of the eighteenth century did anyone deny in print that God's creation was in perfect harmony with his goodness, but the conclusion Pope drew from that base was sometimes not granted because of what it implied about God's freedom to will something other than what exists. To be sure, there was also a tradition of concluding that this evidently imperfect world could not be the product of a perfect creator. The writers who concluded thus extend from Lucretius through Pierre Bayle, the historical lexicographer who had recently revived the Manichean heresy in his dictionary because the evident evil in the world required explanation. Still, such iconoclastic writers would never have confessed Pope's premises. Surely, then, Pope's argument must be aimed at believers who do not believe far enough. Pope's mentor, Henry St. John, Viscount Bolingbroke, hinted at one worthy candidate in his letter to Jonathan Swift of 2 August 1731.

[Pope] pleads the cause of God, I use Seneca's Expression, against that famous charge which atheists in all ages have brought, the supposed unequal Dispensations of Providence, a charge which I cannot heartily forgive you Divines for admitting. you admit it indeed for an extream good purpose, and you build on this admission the necessity of a future state of Rewards & punishments. But what if you should find that this future state will not account for Gods justice, in the present state, which you give up, in opposition to the atheist? would it not have been better to defend God's justice in this world against these daring men by irrefragable Reasons, and to have rested the proof of the other point on Revelation?[6]

These divines fit Pope's specifications particularly well, although some deists and supposed atheists share with them the argument that a future life is necessary to make retribution for the obvious limitations of this one.

By far the most popular way to account for the apparent evil in the world was the one Pope used: Human conclusions about evil are the product of human fallibility of observation; partial evil is universal good, or apparent evil is actual good. These arguments all use the basic notion that if evil did exist, its presence could be determined only by observing the purposive working of the entire system in which individual actions take place. Some writers, however, accepted the reality of evil in the world (that is, they did not explain evil away as an illusion or a trick of false perspective) and used the existence of this actual evil as proof of human immortality. If God is known to be benevolent and yet evils exist, the argument ran, then evils must be compensated in some other sphere of existence. This is, of course, an argument that infinite attributes must form the best world; therefore, this imperfect world must be supplemented by another. The author of *Two Letters from a Deist*, supposedly one Nicholas Stevens, gives the argument in support of a sys-

6. Sherburn, 3:214.

tem which the book's editor called atheistic,[7] though, as the title indicates, Stevens thought of himself as a deist.

As to God's benevolence, this world consider'd by itself certainly does not shew it; and indeed if this world be made without any regard to another state, I cannot help thinking of the moral world, as *Alphonsus* was said to have done of the natural, that 'tis a very bungling piece of workmanship. Hence I conclude, that as surely as God is a wise Being, so sure is it that this world has respect to something else.[8]

Whatever Stevens' secret purposes may have been in introducing such an argument, more orthodox writers such as William Sherlock[9] and Archbishop Tillotson found it useful as well.

The Dispensations of God's Providence in this world, toward good and bad Men, are many times very promiscuous, and very cross, and contrary to what might be expected from the Wise and Just Sovereign of the World, from one whom we believe to love Righteousness, and to hate Iniquity. For Virtuous and Holy Men are often ill treated in this World, grievously harassed and afflicted, and that *for Righteousness sake:* and bad Men many times flourish and are prosperous, *they are not in trouble like other Men, neither are they plagued like other Men.* And this is a very great Objection against the Providence of God; if there were no other consideration had of Virtue and Vice, no other kind of Retribution made to good and bad Men, but what we see in this World. And therefore the Justice of the Divine Providence seems to require, that there should be a day of Recompence, and a solemn and publick Distribution of Rewards and Punishments to the Righteous and to the Wicked. For this is plainly a state of trial and probation, of patience, and forbearance to Sinners,

7. The work is attributed to Nicholas Stevens by Halkett and Laing and the British Museum Catalogue, where the editor is identified as Samuel Wesley.

8. Nicholas Stevens, *Two Letters From a Deist to His Friend, Concerning the Truth and Propagation of Deism, In Opposition to Christianity. With Remarks* (London, 1730), p. 5.

9. William Sherlock, *A Discourse Concerning the Divine Providence* (London, 1694), p. 220. This work was a classic and had gone through six editions by 1725. Sherlock uses the usual arguments to explain evil away as well.

and of exercise to good Men; and being a state of trial, it is not so proper a Season for the distribution of publick Justice. But since the Justice of God doth not appear in this World, it seems very reasonable to believe, that there will be a time when it will be made manifest, and every eye shall see it; that God will one day fully vindicate his Righteousness, and acquit the honour of his Justice. . . .[10]

This is clearly the argument Bolingbroke had in mind, though Tillotson need not be his target, and the line of reasoning that Pope follows is intended to counter such an argument. Pope specifically denies the inequality of dispensations and therefore the validity of the argument that unequal dispensations are an observable flaw in need of correction. Characteristically, he uses two methods. In the lines from the first epistle just quoted he uses the a priori argument, and in the fourth epistle he turns the whole argument in a different direction. He does not deny that good men suffer and evil men prosper. Instead, he denies that their dispensation comes to them because they are good or evil.

10. John Tillotson, Works (London, 1722), 2:141. It may be best to leave Pope's antagonist open here to whoever accepted both parts of his argument but denied his conclusion. One of his most important points, his denial of reason as man's predominant motivation, may be taken as a refutation of both deists and some of the orthodox rationalists. The twentieth-century student should exercise caution in deciding who was a deist and who was not according to the logical necessity of arguments, but the writers of the time were not particularly careful in this regard. Latent deism was as dangerous to them as actual deism, and arguments which led toward the conclusion that reason unaided by revelation could discover either the necessary forms of worship or the necessary moral law were threatening, no matter how piously they were expressed.

Of the handful of arguments involved in the deist controversy from Herbert of Cherbury to Tindal, one of particular interest to readers of the Essay on Man reached a culmination in 1730 when Daniel Waterland wrenched the issue away from the capacity of human reason to discover truth by insisting that what mattered was not what man could know but what motivated him. The argument of either actual deists or the orthodox who seemed headed toward deism by logical extension of their arguments was thus punctured by Waterland's forceful (though not original, except in emphasis) insistence that man is motivated by self-love, not by abstract truth; therefore, authority capable of inflicting rewards and punishments is necessary to compel man to act according to the moral law, no matter how he may come to know what the moral law is.

A similar example of Pope's speaking to an antagonist who is guilty of certain explicit errors of reasoning rather than to the listening world at large is to be found in lines 134–64 of the first epistle. A prideful reasoner contends that the earth was created for his use, though he also cries, "If Man's unhappy, God's unjust." The trouble with this antagonist's argument is that he assumes man to be a special creature. Therefore, he concludes that the creation should provide for man in a special way. A fuzzy distinction between natural and moral evil results. This antagonist is related to the divine suggested above (if he is not the same) who does not carry his own arguments far enough because he insists that he sees a fault in the system: man suffers ill effects from a mechanism that in all other ways is agreed to be excellent or even perfect. Pope asks him to be consistent in his reasoning and not to rely on the notion that man is a special creature who should be granted exceptions to the rules of the world. Should not the arguer, Pope asks, by the same argument, object to the existence of natural evil?

> But errs not Nature from this gracious end,
> From burning suns when livid deaths descend,
> When earthquakes swallow, or when tempests sweep
> Towns to one grave, whole nations to the deep?
> "No ('tis reply'd) the first Almighty Cause
> "Acts not by partial, but by gen'ral laws;
> "Th' exceptions few; some change since all began,
> "And what created perfect?"—Why then Man?
>
> (I, 141–48)

This rather strange arguer, then, admits that the world is the best possible, "where all must full or not coherent be,/And all that rises, rise in due degree," for he grants that God acts by general laws. Again, this is a good deal to grant, and an atheistic antagonist would demand that Pope assume the burden of proof; but Pope's antagonist does grant all these premises and is misled only in the conclusion. In this case the proper conclusion is that natural and moral evil should both be accounted for as evils of defect. Certainly many divines refused to allow such an accounting because they insisted that God was thereby given responsibility for moral evil, and moral evil must stem from man as a free creature. Pope's position, apparently, is that if one were to make a special case of man, there would then be a defect in the creation. If providence must intervene to protect man, then man is not appropriate for those surroundings into which he was created. In such a case man would actually not be what he should be; for what man should be can be determined only by reference to the system he inhabits.

These two examples of Pope's explicit adjustment of his argument to a single specific issue underline the importance to the reader of determining where the issues lie in any group of assertions. They demonstrate that in the writings of Pope's contemporaries a rather complex set of commonplaces could be accepted by men who were arguing on opposite sides of a basic issue. The actual disagreement of such combatants is bared only when the vital point at issue is exposed. It is, therefore, particularly important when dealing with the *Essay on Man* to isolate the points at issue and determine Pope's position at the crux of argument.

2

The Best of Possible Worlds

The starting point of Pope's systematic vindication of the ways of God to man is the assertion that the existent world is the best which was possible to infinite wisdom and that the form of the creation is a coherent chain of being. Everything that follows in the *Essay on Man* comes more or less directly from the a priori assertion implied in the following fragment:

> Of Systems possible, if 'tis confest
> That Wisdom infinite must form the best,
> Where all must full or not coherent be,
> And all that rises, rise in due degree. . . .
>   (I, 43–46)

At the outset, then, Pope is on controversial ground, for well before Voltaire's humanitarian objection to the apparent complacency in the assertion that this is "the best of all possible worlds," the idea that the existent world could satisfactorily be described by that phrase was subject to earnest attack. The idea that the world is the best possible one is a particularly informative example of that troublesome and slippery concept called by A. O. Lovejoy a "unit idea." The range of contexts contemporary with Pope through which the idea was used shows that it was a virtually neutral assertion, though, nonetheless, a volatile one; for its whole force changed radically with a variation in the system that supported, defended, and explained it. Implied in the idea as some writers saw it was the accompanying ramification that when reason ruled choice and there was in the things to be chosen any inherent or intrinsic excellence, the words *free will* had no real application. Nor was this tangle of implications the result of weak popularizing. Three of the most important philosophers of the period asserted that the world was the best possible, but the varying implications put on the assertion by their larger systems of thought quite transformed the idea, and each decided the issue of free will in a different way.

At one extreme, the freedom of God's will is asserted by René Descartes, who insists that the creation was a matter of arbitrary choice. God is capable of doing anything. No consideration dictates his choice. His acts are arbitrary will. He wills that something be the best at the same time that he wills it shall exist. God must form the best possible world because by definition what God does is best. The world is the best world because he created it. Benedict Spinoza, at the opposite pole, denies any meaning to the concept of freedom as applied to God. The nature of God and of things is so closely bound together that, in order for anything in the world to have been different, God would have to have been different as well. Of course, then, the world is the best possible and also the only possible. Gottfried Wilhelm von Leibniz's position is between the two extremes. God is primarily reasonable; therefore, the best world will be the one that recommends itself most perfectly to reason. Of two possibilities God will always choose the one that is most reasonable; there must be a sufficient reason for him to do anything. If, then, God *must* choose one set of possibilities, the necessity is moral and unobjectionable.

Obviously, then, to three major philosophical minds, the same assertion carried substantially different weight, depending upon where it came from and where it was supposed to lead. The example is of sufficient importance to warrant a more detailed discussion. Ralph Cudworth, the influential Cambridge Platonist, reacted to Descartes' system in a way that clarifies the issues and demonstrates one important school of contemporary commentary.

> *Ren. Cartesius,* (though otherwise an Acute Philosopher) was here
> no less *Childish,* in affirming, that all things whatsoever, even the
> Natures of *Good and Evil,* and all *Truth* and *Falshood,* do so depend
> upon the *Arbitrary Will* and *Power of God,* as that if he had pleased,
> *Twice Two should not have been Four,* nor the *Three Angles of a
> Plain Triangle, Equal to Two Right ones,* and the like: he only adding, that all these things notwithstanding, when they were once
> settled by the Divine Decree, became *Immutable.* . . .[1]

Cudworth's comparison of moral realities with supposed mathematical or geometrical realities reflects a desire to arrive at mathematical certainty in moral or philosophical propositions that is frequently to be encountered throughout the fifty years that followed his work. The school of thought that attempted to found moral obligation upon natural relationships between things found this mathematical certainty particularly convincing. In the present quotation Cudworth is censuring Descartes' notion of will, for to Cudworth omnipotence does not mean "capable of anything"; even to omnipotence, only that is possible which is "Conceivable, and Implies no manner of Contradiction."[2] Cudworth's solution to God's apparent lack of freedom, in the case where he must form the best world,

1. Ralph Cudworth, *The True Intellectual System of the Universe* (London, 1678), p. 646.
2. Ibid., p. 647.

introduces problems of its own, but it is not necessary to deal with them here because the conclusion that moral obligation does not eliminate free will is more clearly delineated by Leibniz.

In his sixth "Meditation," Descartes says that the essence of human liberty is the ability to act with the clear recognition of what is true and good.

Hence this indifference which I feel, when I am not swayed to one side rather than to the other by lack of reason, is the lowest grade of liberty, and rather evinces a lack or negation in knowledge than a perfection of will: for if I always recognized clearly what was true and good, I should never have trouble in deliberating as to what judgment or choice I should make, and then I should be entirely free without ever being indifferent.[3]

In the sixth set of objections to the *Meditations* (objections "urged by divers Theologians and Philosophers"),[4] the writers object to the notion that indifference is not a part of the best kind of freedom, for they are sure that God was indifferent in some things, and that, therefore, God's liberty would be of an inferior kind according to Descartes' position.

But do you not see [the objectors continue] that by positing this you destroy the liberty of God, from Whom you remove that indifference as to whether He will create this world rather than another or any world at all? Though yet it belongs to the faith to believe that God has from eternity been indifferent as to whether He would create one, or many, worlds, or no world. But who doubts that God has at all times had the clearest vision of all things that were to be done or left undone? Therefore the clearest vision and perception of things does not annul the indifference of choice; and if it cannot harmonize with human liberty, neither will it be compatible with the divine, since the essences of things are, like numbers, indivisible and unchanging. Wherefore indifference is included no less in the divine than in human freedom of choice.[5]

3. René Descartes, *The Philosophical Works,* trans. Elizabeth S. Haldane and G. R. T. Ross (Cambridge, 1931), 1:175.

4. Ibid., 2:234, n. 1.

5. Ibid., 2:237.

In his reply to this objection Descartes gives his view of why God selected the world we have. He says that it is wrong to judge God's freedom of will by ours in any way. It would also be wrong to say that the idea of good impelled God in his choice.

... God did not will to create the world in time because he saw that it would be better thus than if he created it from all eternity; nor did he will the three angles of a triangle to be equal to two right angles because he knew that they could not be otherwise. On the contrary, because he worked to create the world in time it is for that reason better than if he had created it from all eternity; and it is because he willed the three angles of a triangle to be necessarily equal to two right angles that this is true and cannot be otherwise; and so in other cases. . . . Thus that supreme indifference in God is the supreme proof of his omnipotence.[6]

One objection to this view of God's motivation was that if God is thus capricious nothing can be depended on. But to Descartes the structure of the universe became necessary only after God created it, and he was not forced to create it as it is out of necessity.[7]

In the fourth "Meditation" Descartes denies that the qualities of the creation (the excellence of each quality) impelled God to create what exists rather than something else. Nevertheless, Descartes is not satisfied with a description of the creation that sounds arbitrary in any unfavorable sense of the word, and he tailors his final position so that he is still able to assert that God "ever wills what is best."

And on considering the nature of God it does not appear to me possible that He should have given me a faculty which is not perfect of its kind, that is, which is wanting in some perfection due to it. For if it is true that the more skilful the artizan, the more perfect is the

6. Ibid., p. 248.

7. See Descartes' letter to Père Mesland of 2 May 1644, where he distinguishes between God's willing something to be necessary and being necessitated to will in a certain way (Descartes, *Oeuvres,* ed. Charles Adam and Paul Tennery [Paris, 1901], 4:118–19).

work of his hands, what can have been produced by this supreme Creator of all things that is not in all its parts perfect? And certainly there is no doubt that God could have created me so that I could never have been subject to error; it is also certain that He ever wills what is best; is it then better that I should be subject to err than that I should not?[8]

In order to walk the narrow line between arbitrary necessity and a chaos negating the existence of God, Descartes says, with Pope, that we may think we see the world badly constructed because we do not see the whole fabric of creation.

It further occurs to me that we should not consider one single creature separately, when we inquire as to whether the works of God are perfect, but should regard all his creations together. For the same thing which might possibly seem very imperfect with some semblance of reason if regarded by itself, is found to be very perfect if regarded as part of the whole universe. . . .[9]

Descartes' handling of this question, then, demonstrates that the assertion that the world is the best possible is not capable of being separated from a context which supplies the answers to other crucial issues: (1) how does the quality of the creation affect God's freedom to give it being; (2) is there any way to determine what *best* might mean? Descartes insists on God's freedom and the consequent arbitrariness of choice; and he, rather uncomfortably, settles the question of relative excellence by asserting that what God forms is best by definition. With his notion that God is analogous to an artisan, however, he is clearly on the verge of admitting that the best is the most skilfully constructed.

A somewhat popularized version of the notion that God's skill would prevent inappropriate productions shows the direction in which the solution leads. God, the argument would go, has certain attributes. Since infinite wisdom is one of those attributes, God will act in accord with that attribute. He might

8. Descartes, *Works,* 1:173.
9. Ibid., pp. 173–74.

be said to be compelled by that trait, but since the trait is part of himself, he is compelled by himself. Infinite wisdom would be compelled to form the best. It would not be compelled by some force outside of itself that recognizes what is best and compels infinite wisdom to choose that best world. Infinite wisdom chooses the best because it is characteristic of infinite wisdom that it will choose what it perceives to be the best. If one were to apply this scheme to Pope's statement, he might say that God will form the best possible world because God will act like God—not because something forces him to act like God, but because he is God. Cudworth says it succinctly.

Nor is the Deity therefore *Bound* or *Obliged* to do the *Best,* in any way of *Servility* (as men fondly imagine this to be contrary to his *Liberty*) much less by the Law and Command of any Superiour (which is a Contradiction) but only by the *Perfection* of its own *Nature,* which it cannot possibly deviate from, no more than Ungod it self.[10]

What these quotations, and the ones that follow, demonstrate is that the issue is not over the actual qualities of the creation. These are apparently agreed upon. The sole issue is the source of God's motivation, for if the source is in any way external and resident in the creation, then the creator's relation-

10. Cudworth, p. 874. Cf. also Samuel Clarke, "A Demonstration of the Being and Attributes of God," in Samson Letsome and John Nicholl, eds., *A Defense of Natural and Revealed Religion; Being a Collection of the Sermons preached at the Lecture founded by the Honourable Robert Boyle, Esq.,* 3 vols. (London, 1739), 2:52 (hereafter cited as BLS). (Note that the last Boyle lecture took place in 1732, and most were published at the time of the lecture.)

Some confusion in this general way of looking at the problem is noted by Edmund Law, editor and translator of William King's *Essay on the Origin of Evil,* in a note in King's work: ". . . No *limits* or defect can be apply'd to *either* his Existence or Power. For *Limitation* is an *effect* of some *superior cause.* . . . To suppose this Being limited *in* or *by* its own *Nature,* is to suppose some *Nature antecedent,* or *limiting Quality superior,* to that Being. . . ." ([London, 1731], p. 46.) But Law also limits this view: "Yet, we have as great an Assurance that there are Moral Qualities in God, and that he will always Act according to these Moral Qualities, as the nature of the thing admits . . ." (ibid., p. 47).

ship ceases to be transcendental and free and becomes bound
to the creation in such a way that the creation exerts its own
force of necessity. The same issue plays a role in moral and
political theorizing, as well as in theological. In both religious
and political controversy the key issue frequently goes unstated,
but one observation is the fulcrum upon which many a system
turns: If man's ideas and perceptions are an accurate standard
for judgments of goodness or badness (that is, if the qualities
attached to things are inherent in them so that men may see
them) then supreme, extrahuman authority is unnecessary in
either church or state because all questions can be answered by
self-evident logical demonstrations. Any claim, then, to implicit
faith or obedience is spurious, since explicit proof is always
available.[11]

Spinoza, as he opposes Descartes, does not regard freedom of
will as any positive value. He objects to a separation of God,
as creator, from the creation. This separation is evident in all
systems of thought where God is associated with any sort of
choice or will. To Spinoza, God is immanent in the creation
and does not exist apart from it. Indeed, there is but one thing,
and that is God. Spinoza disagrees specifically with Descartes.

There are some who think that God is a free cause because He can,
as they think, bring about that those things which we have said follow
from His nature—that is to say, those things which are in His power
—should not be, or should not be produced by Him. But this is
simply saying that God could bring about that it should not follow
from the nature of a triangle that its three angles should be equal to
two right angles, or that from a given cause an effect should not
follow, which is absurd.[12]

To Spinoza everything exists out of the necessity of its being
and the being of the divine nature. "In nature there is nothing
contingent, but all things are determined from the necessity of

11. Note the discussion below (pp. 115–25), where the issue is effectively
changed from what man knows to what motivates him.
12. Benedict Spinoza, *The Philosophy of Spinoza, Selected from his Chief
Works*, ed. Joseph Ratner (New York, 1927), p. 132 (*Ethics*, Prop. 17).

the divine nature to exist and act in a certain manner."[13] This, of course, means that there is no question of choice at all, and terms like *possible* and *best* are replaced by *necessary*.

All things have necessarily followed from the given nature of God and from the necessity of His nature have been determined to existence and action in a certain manner. If therefore things could have been of another nature, or could have been determined in another manner to action, so that the order of nature would have been different, the nature of God might then be different to that which it now is, and hence that different nature would necessarily exist, and there might consequently be two or more Gods, which is absurd. Therefore things could be produced by God in no other manner and in no other order than that in which they have been produced.[14]

To many of Pope's contemporaries any restriction on God's freedom of choice ran the danger of involving God so thoroughly with the creation that he could not finally be distinguished from it. For this reason an assertion that involved any kind of necessity was to them a step toward an inevitable atheism; the necessity that was *Spinozism* could be scented at a good many removes from the actual assertions of Spinoza.

Leibniz attempted a path between the extremes of arbitrariness and necessity. His correspondence with Samuel Clarke was published in 1717. Clarke, though now obscured by time, was widely considered by his contemporaries to be the great English philosophical mind of the age. The correspondence between the two grew out of Leibniz' objection to the idea (he attributed it to Newton and his followers) that the physical world was not made a perfectly functioning machine, so that God must intervene "to *wind up* his Watch from Time to Time." Leibniz objects, "He had not, it seems, sufficient Foresight to make it a perpetual Motion."[15] Leibniz asserted that

13. Ibid., p. 135 (*Ethics*, Prop. 29).

14. Ibid., p. 136 (*Ethics*, Prop. 33).

15. Samuel Clarke, *A Collection of Papers which Passed between the Late Learned Mr. Liebnitz, and Dr. Clarke, in the Years 1715 and 1716. Relating to the Principles of Natural Philosophy and Religion* (London, 1717), p. 5.

this is the best possible world, and God was to him a totally reasonable being. He could not accept the notion that God would have made a world containing malfunctions which he must intervene to set right.

The basic question here remains the same. Why did God create the world as it is? Leibniz says that God created it because it was the best possible world. He rejects the notion of sheer will because by his definition God (who is characterized largely by reason) could do nothing without a sufficient reason. Clarke agrees with Leibniz' general principle of sufficient reason, but he says that "this *sufficient Reason* is oft-times no other, than the *mere Will* of God."[16] To Leibniz such a statement is a perversion of the words involved. The act of willing in God would not take place without a sufficient reason to motivate it. Where there is no preference based on reason there would be no act of will.

This concept was troublesome to Clarke. He could not deny that God would always choose the best, for to deny it would be to deny God infinite goodness. On the other hand, if God always chooses the best, how can it be said that God is free? Clarke's solution was to introduce a new group of ideas into the plan. Clarke's claim is not that God always acts out of sheer will. "Undoubtedly nothing *is,* without a *sufficient* Reason *why* it *is,* rather than *not;* and *why* it is *Thus,* rather than *Otherwise.* But in things in their own Nature indifferent; *mere Will,* without any thing External to influence it, is alone *That sufficient Reason.*"[17] Clarke does not go into detail here, but it appears that he describes three orders of possible objects: good, which God will choose because they are good; bad, which God will reject because they are bad; and indifferent, which God will choose as it strikes his fancy to do so.[18] Therefore, one sees in Clarke a further sort of assertion that things are good be-

16. Ibid., pp. 37–39.

17. Ibid., p. 73.

18. King makes use of a similar distinction for man but leaves God indifferent toward objects and, consequently, free (King, pp. 197ff.).

cause God chooses them, rather than that he chooses them be-
cause they are good. Leibniz, however, rejects Clarke's shift by moving the principle of sufficient reason one step further back and by attempting to take the discussion out of the realm of speculation. Leibniz says that in fact no two things do exist that are precisely the
same or which are indifferent, and they do not exist because
of the principle of sufficient reason. Once a specific thing is in
existence there would be no sufficient reason for making another just like it. No two things exactly alike, then, do exist;
and if in speculation one can conceive of two indifferent concepts, he may be sure that neither would be brought into existence because there would be no sufficient reason for making the
choice.

Clarke cannot accept the explanation (he regards it as the-
oretical) and insists that God must be allowed to choose in
some areas or else be governed by fate. Here Leibniz tries a new
attack, largely a semantic one. Clarke, he feels, is perverting
the word *choose,* for when we say that a being chooses, we
mean that he acts according to a reason he knows and clearly
prefers (notice the similarity to Descartes' idea discussed
above).

As for *Moral* Necessity, This also does not derogate from *Liberty.*
For when a Wise Being, and especially God, who has Supreme
Wisdom, chuses what is Best, he is not the less free upon that account:
On the contrary, it is the most perfect Liberty, not to be hindered
from acting in the best manner. And when Any Other chuses according to the most apparent and the most strongly inclining Good, he
imitates therein the Liberty of a truly Wise Being, in proportion to
his disposition. Without this, the Choice would be a blind Chance.[19]

It is only when a being has no reason, no motivation to action,
when he moves without knowing what causes him to move,
that he may be said to be unfree. Leibniz confesses, however,
that such a concept may possibly be called a kind of fatalism.

19. Samuel Clarke, *Collection,* p. 159.

He earlier made a distinction between different kinds of fatalism, and the moral necessity referred to in the foregoing quotation is the key to his concept.

We must also distinguish between a *Necessity*, which takes place because the Opposite implies a Contradiction; (which necessity is called *Logical, Metaphysical,* or *Mathematical*;) and a *Necessity* which is *Moral*, whereby a Wise Being chuses the Best, and every Mind follows the strongest Inclination.[20]

If this is necessity, it is an unobjectionable variety. " 'Tis not *This Fatality,* (which is only the wisest Order of Providence) but a *Blind Fatality* or *Necessity*, void of All Wisdom and Choice which we ought to avoid."[21]

Leibniz, too, says that God is limited to what is possible, but within existent possibilities can effect any of them. It is because he can effect any possibility that he can actually be said to choose among them. Leibniz meets the possible objection (that if God must form the best, then there is only one possible world because its superiority is part of its possibility) by asking for a more accurate use of words. It is inaccurate to apply the word *necessary* to God's choosing the best world, "for, what is *necessary,* is so by its Essence, since the Opposite implies a Contradiction; But a Contingent which exists, owes its Existence to the *Principle of what is Best,* which is a *sufficient Reason* for the Existence of Things."[22]

Probably the most striking similarity between the conclusions of Pope and Leibniz is their reliance on wisdom as God's governing trait. If some of Pope's contemporaries could suggest that God's creation at times called his attributes into question, it was never all of the creation or all of God's attributes that came into conflict. The doubtful did not ask in a general manner how God could create this world, but how a God who is infinitely good or benevolent could have produced a world where evil and malevolence exist. God's attributes frequently

20. Ibid., p. 157.
21. Ibid., p. 63.
22. Ibid., p. 161.

set up apparently conflicting demands so that to act according to infinite mercy and infinite justice at the same time appeared too much of a challenge even for infinite insight. Pope and Leibniz meet this problem in a similar manner. They assign to God a predominant attribute which determines all conflicting cases by its superior position. Wisdom sets the standards by which other attributes are to be measured. Pope and Leibniz have, thereby, redefined the key terms and hidden the original question.

Presumably the original charge against God was that there is pain in the world, and there would not be pain in the best world, or in a world created by infinite goodness. Pope says, as to some extent Leibniz does as well, that the best world is not a painless one, but one "Where all must full or not coherent be,/ And all that rises, rise in due degree." The best system is the one that functions most accurately, with everything in its place and a place for everything. If this accurate functioning engenders pain, as it does, then the world is still the best possible because that degree of pain was unavoidable. A man who complains of his own misery is impiously suggesting that God, merely in order to save men some pain, should have destroyed the intricate fabric of the whole.

There was, however, even among those writers who attributed to God one predominant attribute, considerable difference of opinion as to which of God's attributes should be said to predominate. Edmund Law, the translator and editor of the English edition of King's *Essay on the Origin of Evil*, states, in a note to King's text, what is to him the orthodox view of the proper emphasis. "Thus may we reason about the several perfections of the supreme Being, but that which should chiefly direct us in these our Enquiries, is the Idea of his *Infinite Goodness*."[23] Joseph Butler (later the author of *The Analogy of Religion Natural and Revealed* and Bishop of Durham) in his *Fifteen Sermons Preached at the Rolls Chapel*, in 1726, gives his

23. King, p. 48.

support to goodness as the proper motivation to assign to God: ". . . Perfect goodness in the Deity is the principle from whence the universe was brought into being, and by which it is preserved. . . ."[24] Archbishop Tillotson expressed the same opinion earlier, defending the existence of goodness as an attribute of God and warning of the danger inherent in isolated wisdom. (Pope does not deny the goodness of God merely by stressing his wisdom; however, granting that both traits exist, many writers apparently believed that God was maligned by a writer who said that wisdom overruled goodness in the divine character.) Tillotson says, "Knowledge and power are great perfections, but separated from goodness, they would be great imperfections, nothing but craft and violence."[25] John Wilkins, Bishop of Chester, expressed the idea more fully.

Knowledge and *Power* without *Goodness,* would be but *craft* and *violence.* He can by his *Wisdom* out-wit his Creatures, and easily impose upon them; and by his *Power* he could tyrannize over them, and play with their misery; but that he will not do thus, we are assured by his *Goodness.*[26]

Bishop Wilkins' warning is interesting to Pope's readers because in the *Essay* God does in a sense outwit his creatures so that the purposes of the whole will be fulfilled whether the creature intends that they should be or not.

> . . . HEAV'N's great view is One, and that the Whole:
> That counter-works each folly and caprice;
> That disappoints th' effect of ev'ry vice. . . .
>   (II, 238–40)

It may well be that, as Wilkins describes God, goodness would prevent him from making human beings do what is good with-

24. Joseph Butler, *The Works of Bishop Butler,* ed. J. A. Bernard (London, 1900), 1:102.

25. John Tillotson, *The Works of the Most Reverend Dr. John Tillotson, Late Lord Archbishop of Canterbury,* ed. Ralph Barker, 3rd ed. (London, 1722), 1:679.

26. John Wilkins, *Of the Principles and Duties of Natural Religion,* 4th ed. (London, 1699), p. 138–39.

out their knowing what they are doing. Such goodness is not what makes Pope's system operate.

King, too, in contrast to Pope, puts stress on God's goodness as the motivation for the creation (wisdom playing its part in achieving what goodness demands).

And hence it manifestly follows, that the World is as well as it could be made by infinite *Power* and *Goodness*. For since the Exercise of the Divine Power, and the Communication of his Goodness, are the Ends for which the World is fram'd, there is no doubt but God has attain'd these Ends.[27]

Pope's whole manner of defending the creation is based upon the asserted transcendence of the system as a whole over the isolated functioning of any parts. The danger of turning God into a sadistic mechanic by this method is considerable. No author of any influence attacks God's benevolent motivation, however, though some seemed, to contemporary analysis, to do so by the logical demands of their argument. In fact, the argument that God acts by *general* laws for the *general* good was usually fortified by an assurance that the world is benevolent as well as perfect in its mechanics and that God's wisdom is enlightened by goodness. For Pope and Leibniz, however, were wisdom and goodness to come into conflict, wisdom would decide the outcome.

The implications of his choice of wisdom as God's dominant attribute did not elude Pope. He does describe the world in terms of inevitable mechanical forces and demands. The form taken by the best possible world in order to meet the requirements of infinite wisdom is the persistent image elaborated in Lovejoy's *The Great Chain of Being*. The universe is a chainlike series of interdependencies where every link must exist in order to maintain the continuity and the very existence of the whole. The links are logically and mechanically necessary as a result of some characteristic or group of characteristics inher-

27. King, p. 53. For a more detailed identification of King, see below, chap. 3, pp. 56–57.

ent in each link. Not only was Pope aware of the necessity, he explicitly includes it in his system. Man is a test case, and in answer to the supposed assertion that a benevolent God would either have improved or omitted this suffering link, Pope insists that, logically, no such alteration was possible.

> On superior pow'rs
> Were we to press, inferior might on ours:
> Or in the full creation leave a void,
> Where, one step broken, the great scale's destroy'd:
> From Nature's chain whatever link you strike,
> Tenth or ten thousandth, breaks the chain alike.
> And if each system in gradation roll,
> Alike essential to th' amazing whole;
> The least confusion but in one, not all
> That system only, but the whole must fall.
> Let Earth unbalanc'd from her orbit fly,
> Planets and Suns run lawless thro' the sky,
> Let ruling Angels from their spheres be hurl'd,
> Being on being wreck'd, and world on world,
> Heav'n's whole foundations to their centre nod,
> And Nature tremble to the throne of God. . . .
>   (I, 241–56)

To be sure, Pope deals with the excellence of man's present structure at length, but dialectically man exists in the creation because he is necessary to the cohesion of the functioning system. Compare King's argument on the same point:

But you may wish that some other Place and Condition had fallen to your Lot; perhaps so: but if you had taken up another's Place, that other, or some else, must have been put into yours, who, being alike ungrateful to the Divine Providence, would wish for the Place which you now have occupied. Know then that it was necessary that you should either be what you are, or not at all. For since every other Place and State which the System or Nature of Things allow'd, was occupied by some others, you must of necessity either fill that which you now are in, or be banish'd out of Nature. For, do you expect that any other should be turn'd out of his Order, and you placed in his Room? that is, that God should exhibit a peculiar and extraordinary

Munificence toward you to the prejudice of others. You ought therefore not to censure, but adore the Divine Goodness for making you what you are. You could neither have been made otherwise, nor in a better Manner, but to the Disadvantage of some others, or of the whole.[28]

Pope and King agree that man must necessarily be what he is, but King's alternative is nonexistence for man rather than chaos for the entire world. To King, God was motivated to the creation of the world by his desire to produce all possible good. Man as a species was necessary, by this explanation, because of the good that he includes, a quantity of good that otherwise would have been left unrealized. King is, therefore, left with a far less dramatic alternative to omitting man from the scheme of things than the one just quoted from Pope.

If you say, God might have omitted the more imperfect Beings, I grant it, and if that had been best he would undoubtedly have done it. But it is the part of infinite Goodness to choose the very best; from thence it proceeds therefore, that the more imperfect Beings have Existence; for it was agreeable to that, not to omit the very least Good which could be produced.[29]

To neither King nor Pope does man's nature suggest that he should be either improved or omitted from the system of the creation. Both are prepared to defend man's actual excellence and, indeed, his happiness; but when the clearest issue is isolated, the question is, *if* man *were* imperfect, would necessity still demand his existence? Since King says that God was motivated by the latent goodness in the creature, his answer is no; but God, according to Pope, is motivated by the wisdom expressed in coherence and fullness. Man as a possible link in the chain would, therefore, have to be created to hold the whole thing together even if men isolated from the system might be judged to be imperfect or vulnerable. The difference between the two writers' conclusions is partly attributable to the pur-

28. Ibid., p. 125.
29. Ibid., p. 93.

poses of their works. They have much in common, but Pope writes to lower man by attacking his pride, while King intends to be inspirational and elevating. Pope is willing to have man think of himself as a mere cog in a complex machine, but to King the mechanical excellence of the machine is not what justifies its existence. The machine exists because it has more good in it than any other would have had, and the good is moral rather than mechanical.

> . . . 'Tis certain that God was not compell'd by any necessity to create any thing at all, he might therefore have prevented all Moral Evils, if he had not endow'd any Being with Free Choice; for so there would have been nothing that could sin. But such a monstrous Defect and *Hiatus* would have been left in Nature by this means, *viz.* by taking away all Free Agents, as would put the World into a worse Condition than that which it is in at present, with all the Moral Evils that attend it, tho' they were multiply'd to a much greater Number.[30]

The specific question of God's freedom is present only by implication in Pope, but it is the primary concern of the largest and most individual part of King's work. King's ideas on the origin of evil and its relationship to the demands of a complex system are not unusual, but his method of demonstrating God's freedom of choice is his most singular cluster of ideas. He works out an elaborate demonstration of freedom as it exists in the world in order that he may compensate for the inherent fatalism of his system. For with all his assurance of the excellence of the world, King sees that to make the excellence of the creation the reason for its existence is to deprive God of the freedom of choosing another possibility.

> We must not therefore attend to such as declare that God chooses things because they are Good, as if Goodness and the greater Good, which he perceives in Objects, could determine his will.[31]

His conclusion is that "God, by willing, makes those things pleasing to him which were before indifferent."[32] For, King in-

---

30. Ibid., p. 229.
31. Ibid., p. 186.
32. Ibid., p. 187.

sists, if there were any reason why God produced external things " 'tis manifest, that, according to this, all things will proceed from him necessarily."[33]

But if things be good and agreeable to God for this only reason, because he has chosen to make them so, he himself will be at liberty, his whole Work will be free. The World will be produced, not by necessity, but choice; neither will it be impossible to be effected, tho' it be in itself unprofitable to the Deity, for he will have a complacency in his own Choice. And from hence it sufficiently appears of how great importance it is, that all the Goodness of the Creatures should depend on the Divine Election, and not that upon the Goodness of them, for we see that by this means Fate is destroy'd, and Liberty establish'd.[34]

King maintains that we ought not to inquire into the reason for God's election because if there was a reason there was no freedom. "For if we suppose that there is such a thing as better and worse in the Objects themselves, who would affirm that the Goodness and Wisdom of God will not necessarily determine him to choose the better?"[35] And in what is perhaps the most forceful statement of his position, he says, "Nay so great is the Power of God, that whatever he shall choose out of infinite Possibilities, that will be the best, it matters not therefore which he prefers."[36]

Then, however, King makes a distinction similar to that of Descartes mentioned above. He divides elections into primary and subsequent. He posits thereby the notion that while God may act with indifference and out of sheer will when electing to create anything, subsequent elections regarding the system into which that thing fits, or the attributes of the thing itself, are not absolutely free.

For when we conceive any thing proposed to the Knowledge of God as fit to be done, he must also necessarily have under his Eye, as it

33. Ibid., p. 188.
34. Ibid.
35. Ibid., p. 190.
36. Ibid.

were at the same Glance, all those things that are necessarily connected with it, or consequent thereupon to all Eternity; and must
will or reject them all by one simple Act. If therefore he determin'd
to create Man, he must also be supposed to will that he should consist
of a Soul and Body, that he should be furnish'd with Reason and
Senses, and that his Body should be subject to the general Laws of
Matter: for all these things are evidently included in the Choice to
create Man.

   Nay this primary Act of Volition must be supposed to contain
not only those things which have a necessary connection with what is
chosen, but such things also as tend to promote its benefit and happiness, as far as they can be made consistent with the benefit of the
whole. For since God is infinitely Good, 'tis certain that he wills
that his Creatures should exist commodiously as much as that they
should exist at all. He therefore will'd such things as are agreeable to
the Natures, and tend to preserve the Constitutions of his Creatures
in the same Election whereby he determin'd to create them.[37]

He goes on to say that there are two kinds of goodness in
things. One is that they conform to God's will, that they are
good because he created them, and the other is that they "promote the Convenience, Preservation and Perfection of the
whole."[38]

   An interpretation of this segment of King's argument gives
an interesting variation on Pope's own statement. King might
say that out of the possible systems (and to him God is limited
by possibilities) there was no quality in any one of them which
made God prefer it to another. The goodness of the present
system is a result of God's having chosen it. However, having
once decided to choose the general nature of the present world
(or perhaps even the nature of one of its inhabitants) God's attributes motivated him to make it the best system out of what
might be considered its own hypothetically possible variations.
There is a sense, then, in which King states that God must *form*
the best system once he has chosen its general outline or any of

37. Ibid., pp. 191–92.
38. Ibid., p. 192.

its parts, and this sort of position could account for Pope's use of the word *form* rather than, say, *choose*.

To King, whatever system God chose would be perfect within its own range of associations and potentialities. Of the infinite possibilities King mentions, each one would entail a system perfectly suited to it. Which perfectly functioning system he might choose is a matter of indifference, and the one that he actually chooses becomes the best by his having chosen it, and by that alone. While King's and Pope's ideas are capable of supporting the same basic conclusion (that the very character of God insures his creation against charges of imperfection), King's qualifications and justifications of his system leave Pope much nearer to the position of Leibniz than to the considerable modifications of King.[39]

In summary, there is a relevant range of adaptations into which the assertion that God must form the best possible world may fit. That range has the following assertions as its extremes. (1) God chooses what he will, and what he chooses becomes the best by virtue of his having chosen it. (2) God's nature and the nature of things together dictate existence, and nothing could be other than it is without altering either one or the other—an alternative both impossible and absurd.

Pope's position is between the two extremes and was already clearly set out by Leibniz (and in more orthodox though less detailed sources such as Cudworth).[40] It is clearly what Leibniz called moral necessity that compelled God in Pope's view, for God acted as he did because of the qualities of what would have been produced if he had acted otherwise.[41] In other words,

39. For a discussion of Pope's indebtedness to Leibniz see C. A. Moore, "Did Leibniz Influence Pope's Essay?" *Journal of English and Germanic Philology* 16 (January 1917):84–102. "From any point of view, the assumption that Pope was necessarily indebted to the *Théodicée* is untenable" (ibid., p. 101).

40. See above, p. 25.

41. It is interesting to note here that granting moral attributes to God was a bête noire of Bolingbroke's, and he wrote with considerable sarcasm to Swift on this argument of Pope's, though its importance to Pope's system

Pope admits necessity of a kind. He frees God of any blame for not having made the creation better, and he glorifies him for having chosen the existent world for its positive excellence rather than its appeal to his arbitrary will. God receives credit for having willed the best, and the creation receives credit for being the best.

---

can hardly be overestimated: "I received some time ago a letter from Dr Delany, & very lately Mr Pope sent me some sheets which seem to contain the substance of two sermons of that gentlemans. the Philosophia prima is above my reach, and especially when it attempts to prove that God has done or does so and so, by attempting to prove that so and so is essential to his attributes or necessary to his design, and that the not doing so and so would be inconsistent with the former or repugnant to the latter. I content my self to contemplate what I am sure He has done, & to adore Him for it in humble Silence" (Sherburn, 3:211).

3

God as the Soul of the World

Despite his description of the best possible creation in terms that appear quite mechanical, Pope's further performance in the poem shows that he was not satisfied with the mechanical description alone but wanted as well to argue that the world is controlled by immanent spirit. For the sake of argument he was willing that his a priori assertions should result in inflexible necessity regarding man's present state. His case is that, should the link that comprises the human species have been omitted from the chain, the entire creation would have fallen into chaos. Most of his attention, however, is directed to showing that even though it is logically necessary to conclude that the primary concern of the creator is with the functioning of the whole creation, the observed world does not require one to separate individual from universal excellence. To be sure, the a priori argument demands that if man as he exists were subject to acknowledged miseries, he would, nevertheless, exist out of a priori necessity; but Pope's case is that existent man is not a botch or a bungle. As a creature, man is in all ways as he should be.

Although the eighteenth-century conclusion that all is as it should be has been, by Voltaire and others, called optimism, it is in no sense, except perhaps technical, optimistic, since the best *possible* world is not assumed to have much similarity to the best conceivable world, or that which might abstractly be the best. Much of what Pope says about man (and he insists that man is what he should be) is no different from the highly negative observations of the most cynical observers of the human condition—except that Pope's conclusions from such observations are not the same. Just as the best possible world may contain friction and pain, the species *man* may be weak and wicked. The best creature is the one that will function best in the specific context for which he is intended.

One important step in meliorating the apparent danger of heartlessness in Pope's rigorous claims about the world is his assertion that God is the soul of the world. Here he calls on an organic rather than a mechanical metaphor to conceptualize the creation. The world is not like a watch. It is like a man, or at least like a creature with both body and soul.

> **All are but parts of one stupendous whole,**
> **Whose body Nature is, and God the Soul. . . .**
> (I, 267–68)

The notion that God is the soul of the world had a long history. Pope knew that the concept was of questionable orthodoxy, but he used it anyway, though he did not intend to appear unorthodox by doing so.

On 3 March 1733, he wrote to John Caryll, pretending that he did not know the true author of the anonymously published first epistle of the *Essay on Man,* and in one of his attempts to equivocate genteelly he noticed that the author of the anonymous poem might be suspected of unorthodoxy because of the assertion that God is the soul of the world.

The town is now very full of a new poem intitled *an Essay on Man,* attributed, I think with reason, to a divine. It has merit in my opinion but not so much as they give it; at least it is incorrect and has some inaccuracies in the expressions; one or two of an unhappy kind, for they may cause the author's sense to be turned, contrary to what I think his intention a little unorthodoxically. Nothing is so plain as that he quits his proper subject, *this present world,* to insert his belief of *a future state* and yet there is an *If* instead of a *Since* that would overthrow his meaning and at the end he uses the Words *God,* the *Soul* of the *World,* which at first glance may be taken for heathenism, while his whole paragraph proves him quite Christian in his system, from *Man* up to *Seraphim.*[1]

Evidently, Pope believed that the context into which the "heathen" notion that God is the soul of the world was placed determined its orthodoxy or lack thereof. The context of his argument is as follows. In section 8 of the first epistle he expatiates on the system of the chain of being and says that the necessity of every link to the whole chain makes man's inclusion unavoidable. In section 9 he gives an analogy for man's desire to have capacities different from those he has. The comparison is to the human body. What if the foot or the eye or ear refused to play its part because it pridefully thought it should be more important in the whole scheme? What if parts refused "to serve mere engines to the ruling mind"? It is equally absurd to resist the conditions created by "The great directing MIND OF ALL . . ." In both the world and man the purpose and direction of the whole come from a mind; therefore, both man and the universe are guided intellectually. Pope then indents for a new paragraph and gives what amounts to a summary view of the

1. Sherburn, 3:354.

world, not in its physical existence (that is, as an interdependent chain of relationships) but in its spiritual formation as it is inhabited by God.

> All are but parts of one stupendous whole,
> Whose body Nature is, and God the soul;
> That, chang'd thro' all, and yet in all the same,
> Great in the earth, as in th' aethereal frame,
> Warms in the sun, refreshes in the breeze,
> Glows in the stars, and blossoms in the trees,
> Lives thro' all life, extends thro' all extent,
> Spreads undivided, operates unspent,
> Breathes in our soul, informs our mortal part,
> As full, as perfect, in a hair as heart;
> As full, as perfect, in vile Man that mourns,
> As the rapt Seraph that adores and burns;
> To him no high, no low, no great, no small;
> He fills, he bounds, connects, and equals all.
>   (I, 267–80)

This image of God inhabiting the world as a soul inhabits its body is not a passing or forgotten metaphor. He uses it again in the third epistle.

> One all-extending, all-preserving Soul
> Connects each being, greatest with the least....
>   (III, 22–23)

In the passage from the first epistle Pope is working with the subject of God's providence, or the attribute called *immensity* ("that he is every place"). As a subject of controversy, the working of providence is similar in some ways to the necessity for God to create the best possible world. There was little or no disagreement that God's influence ruled the world, but the way in which he worked, or the nature of his involvement, was a more complicated subject because of the implications of the various possibilities. Involving God with the functioning of the world could run the danger of making him immediately responsible for its evils. If the evils are the result of the necessary limitations of the creatures who are by definition less perfect than the creator, or if they are the product of inner stresses necessary to the system, then God is at least at a distance from the actual creation of pain or deformity. If, however, God not only created the world to function in the best possible way but also continues to create it in all of its actions as it functions, then each ill may seem the explicit result of God's acting. He is then directly the cause of evil. Yet the alternative separation of God from immediate involvement with the world would make it a spiritless mechanism.

No controversialist was likely to state either of these extreme conclusions or, for that matter, to hold them. Most, however, were ready to hold an adversary responsible for an extreme position which was the logically necessary extension of what he had admitted, whether he carried the argument that far or not. Seldom, if ever, could a reader find an author acknowledging that his own system left the world a meaningless, spiritless mechanism or that it proved God to be responsible for the evils of the world. Though Pope was aware of the dangerous limits to which his assertion that God is the soul of the world could be pushed, he chose to describe the world as being moved from within by constantly functioning intelligence. The troubles that were caused by Pope's position came from God's consequent responsibility for the origin of evil. That difficulty Pope solved by a related argument.

A closer and more detailed examination of the status of the idea that God is the soul of the world will help to determine how Pope was using the concept in the *Essay on Man*. Implied by this idea is the radical assertion that the world is an animal rather than a machine and so has a soul, whether or not the soul is identified with God. The idea was, as Pope acknowledged in his letter to Caryll, a prevalant pagan (that is, pre-Christian and extra-Christian) concept. With varying degrees of approval, writers commonly attributed the idea to Plato, Aristotle, the Stoics, Virgil, and Seneca. To its advantage it was an antimaterialist position and perceived the world to have an inherent spiritual motivation.[2] One could hardly do better than turn to Cudworth's *True Intellectual System of the Universe* to get the full historical panorama of the idea. Cudworth's main objective throughout this work is to demonstrate the world to be an intellectual system, infused with mind, or consciousness, and directed or guided by it. He has reservations about the way in which the idea that God is the soul of the world can be used in a Christian context, but to him the prevalence of the idea in pagan thought represents a *consensus gentium* and, therefore, a degree of proof that the world is an intellectual system.[3]

There were also ancient Christian writings that more or less equivocally held the same doctrine. Richard Burthogge cites Augustine and Origen as examples. In addition, several scriptural texts were open to interpretation at least in the direction of the pagan conclusion. English divines were somewhat chary of expressing the idea, but they found it useful, especially when discussing God's immensity. The consequence was clearly tempting. On the one hand there were God's omnipresence and spirituality. On the other there was much speculation on the ability of spirit to permeate matter. Even though there was some doubt that spirit could involve itself with matter, for those who resolved that it could mysteriously do so, the spirit or soul of man in the material body provided a useful analogy. John Tillotson, on the subject of God's immensity, shows that we know the actuality of his attributes from the natural notions and dictates of our minds.

We find that the Heathen, by the Light of Nature, did attribute this Perfection to God. *Tully* tells us. . . . *That Pythagoras* thought. . . . *That God is as it were a Soul passing through and inspiring all Nature.*[4]

2. Cudworth, pp. 484, 503ff., 593–94. Richard Burthogge, *An Essay Upon Reason, and the Nature of Spirits* (London, 1694), pp. 126f. Thomas Stanley, *The History of Philosophy* (London, 1655–62), pt. 8, pp. 103–119.
3. See especially pp. 484, 503–6, 593–94.
4. Tillotson, *Works*, 2:756.

John Scott, whose *Christian Life* had gone through at least nine editions by 1730, explicates the Bible in a similar manner.

And that [God] is thus *present* with us we have sufficient reason to conclude, not only from the infinite *Plenitude* of his Essence, which being *Self-existent* could not be *bounded* or *limited* by any Cause from without, and therefore must necessarily be *boundless* and *immense;* but also from express Assertions of Scripture which assures us *that his eyes are in every place beholding the evil and the good,* Prov. xv. 3. *That he is a God at hand and not a God afar off; and that no man can hide himself in secret places that he shall not see him; and that he fills heaven and earth.* Jer. xxiii. 23, 24, and that we can go no whither *from his presence,* Psal. cxxxix. 7,8. And that *All things are naked and open to his eyes,* Heb. iv, 13. that is, that the World is *surrounded* and *filled* with his Being, which is both the *Womb* that *contains,* and the *Soul* that *pervades* the Creation; and that being thus *present* with us wherever we are, he must needs be supposed to have a constant *Inspection* over us, and a clear *Sense* and *Perception* of whatsoever we do.[5]

Isaac Barrow, one of the greatest Caroline divines and preachers, quoted Aristotle to compare God in the world with the soul in man.

As God by his presence and influence doth (as the Philosopher speaks) *contain, and keep together the whole frame of things;* so that he withdrawing them, it would fall of itself into corruption and ruine; So doth the soul by its union and secret energy upon the body connect the parts of its body, and preserve it from dissolution, which presently, they being removed, do follow.

As He, in a manner beyond our conception, without any proper extension, or composition of parts doth co-exist with, penetrateth, and passeth through all things; So is she, in a manner also unconceivable, every where present within her bounds, and penetrates all the dimensions of her little world.[6]

5. John Scott, *The Christian Life, from its Beginning, to its Consummation in Glory; Together With The Several Means and Instruments of Christianity conducing thereunto; with Directions for private Devotion and Forms of Prayer fitted to the several States of Christians* (London, 1681), pp. 333–34.
6. Isaac Barrow, *Works,* ed. John Tillotson, 2d ed. (London, 1686), 2:105–6.

Somewhat later, Thomas Stackhouse, whose *Body of Divinity* of 1729 is rather a compendium of earlier works on divinity, also calls upon the ancients to suggest the manner of God's immensity.

To have an infinite Knowledge of all Things which are most secret and hidden; to be able to do all things; to steer and govern the Actions of all Creatures, and to have a constant and watchful Care of them, seems, in all Reason, to require immediate Presence; and accordingly we may observe that the wisest of the *Heathen* World always espoused this Doctrine: *That God is, as it were, a Soul passing through and inspiring all Nature. . . .*[7]

There is, then, whether Pope knew it or not, no very satisfactory ground upon which to decide the orthodoxy of the idea, even if one wished to do so.[8] The writers appear to be more comfortable with a metaphorical or analogical statement than with the assertion that God is the soul of the world.[9] Analogy, however, was an equivocal tool, and could be a method of both eating and having one's cake. One could use an analogy in theological debate and still declare that since it was an analogy rather than a description, the reality to which it referred remained mysterious or unknown, though the functioning of

7. Thomas Stackhouse, *A Complete Body of Divinity* (London, 1729), p. 79.
8. Ibid., p. 236. Other authors, though perhaps less orthodox, are even more enthusiastic in their wording. Edward Herbert, Baron Herbert, *De Veritate*, trans. Meyrick H. Carré (Bristol, 1937), p. 169. George Hakewill, *An Apologie of the Power and Providence of God in the Government of the World* (London, 1627), p. 39. Nicholas Mosley, ΨΥΧΟΣΟΦΙΑ: *Or Natural and Divine Contemplations of the Passions and Faculties of the Soul of Man* (London, 1653), p. 18. Thomas Robinson, *New Observations on the Natural History of this World of Matter* (London, 1696), p. 9. Sir Humphrey Mackworth, *A Discourse By Way of Dialogue Concerning I. Providence. . . .* 2nd ed. (London, 1705), p. 18.
9. Cf. Barrow, 2:97: ". . . for this whole System of things what is it, but one goodly body (as it were) compacted of several members and organs; so aptly compacted together, that each confers its being and its operation to the grace and ornament, to the strength and stability of the whole; One soul (of divine providence)enlivening in a manner and actuating it all?" See also Nicholas Malebranche, *A Treatise of Nature and Grace* (London, 1695), pp. 34, 89.

God that was described was operationally similar to the human one to which it was compared.[10]

To many writers the very basis of the analogy between God in the world and man's soul in his body was offensive. Among these is a group who hold the creation to be a functioning mechanism.[11] To Robert Boyle and Isaac Newton, for example, the operation of the world by general laws does not suggest the operational presence of God except perhaps on miraculous occasions. One wonders if to them the intrusion of a less obedient and tractable spiritual element would not turn scientific expectation into chaos, though presumably they reached their conclusion more inductively. In fact their expressed concern is theological rather than scientific. Making God the soul of the world turns him into the work rather than the worker.

Like these men, Pope could hardly be more insistent that the universe operates by general laws; nevertheless, he does place God within the creation as its soul. The extent to which he confounds the creature and the creator thereby is not easy to determine, but it is doubtful that he overtly does so at all. He nowhere asserts that God's *only* existence is as soul of the world, and he may, therefore, escape some of the supposed danger. The subtlety in Pope's manipulation of the metophorical similarity of the world and man is that he distinguishes between the purposeful movement of the whole creature and the movements of the individual, independent concomitant parts. Both the human soul and God as the soul of the world are involved exclusively with the movement of the whole being, considered as a unit. The parts move by urges of their own, in the man by some such concept as a vegetative soul and in the world by what Pope calls "plastic nature" (both of which will be explained more fully below). Pope's shift here would not have

10. See the discussion of analogy in chapter 4, pp. 77–81.
11. Robert Boyle, *Works,* 6 vols. (London, 1772), 5:163–64. Isaac Newton, *Mathematical Principles,* ed. Florian Cajori (Berkeley, 1934), p. 544 (this citation is from "The General Scholium," added in 1713). Thomas Hobbes, *Leviathan,* chap. 31.

satisfied Boyle, however, for the latter specifically rejected the concept of plastic nature.[12]

Actually these arguments against the idea that God is the soul of the world are of less importance to Pope's whole system than another which is a ramification of the idea. If God is actively included within the world, then he becomes responsible for its evils. These complications arising from describing God as the soul of the world are interestingly illuminated in Richard Burthogge's *An Essay on Reason and the Nature of Spirits,* published in 1694. Burthogge, a physician, was educated at Oxford and Leyden, and he had an active career as a philosopher, though his writings were apparently not very widely known. In this work he is attempting to discuss the way in which mind and matter may be united. He separates pure mind, which is God, from mind working through matter, as, for example, it does in human beings who think or sense only through the organs but whose thought or consciousness is not in its essence organic. He makes reference to ancient notions of the world as body and soul (p. 126ff.) and distinguishes between two modes by which spirit may cause motion or life.

Thus, [Seneca's] *Ratio faciens* is the Idea or Notion of the *Mosaical* Spirit, the true *Natura Naturans,* that concurred to make the World, not in the manner that God himself did, who, in the Mosaical Hypothesis, Acted only as an External Efficient, but in the way that the *Soul* would do in a living Creature, if first by its Plastic vertue it should form all the members of the Body of it, and afterwards, should inform it, and act in it.[13]

Apparently, his main point is that the "Mosaical Spirit" of the Bible is the soul of the world, but Burthogge was less satisfied that the spirit should be thought of as God. He does intend to show that the world has spirit suffused through it, even though he is wary of making the final connection and calling that spirit God. He also says that separate human souls are individualized portions of the soul of the world, just as a single

12. See Boyle, *Works,* 5:241ff.
13. Burthogge, p. 131

organ or mode of sensation in one man is an individualized portion of his whole soul.[14] His primary objective is to prove the existence of spirits, and he gives an elaborate set of case histories of apparitions and witches in order to demonstrate against various philosophers of the age that spirit exists as well as matter and is separate from it, that is, spirit is not a function of matter. His conclusion about the world is an unusually clear and comprehensive description of the world as a physical creature inhabited by a soul.

Now, As all the *Organs* of any Particular Animal, tho' being Compared *one with Another,* they are *several,* not Parts one of Another, but a kind of wholes, and have their several Faculties; yet in respect of the *Body,* they are but *Parts,* and all Influenced by a *Common Principle,* which giveth being to *its* several Faculties, but is none of them it self. Why may not all the *Animals,* themselves (as well the Invisible as the Visible,) that do Exist in the *Universe,* be, in respect of *this* but as so many *Parts,* so many Organs, (some more Simple, others more Compound) Actuated by some *Common Principle* that Penetrates through out *it;* and yet, in Respect *one of Another,* be several *wholes,* that have their several Powers and Faculties? And then, *as* all the Particular Animals would, in truth, be but as so many several Organs Endued with several Faculties, in which the Organ or System of Organs would be the *Body,* the Faculty or System of Faculties the *Soul; so* all of them taken together would be an Entire Body [of the Universe] Actuated by an Universal Principle, (as by a Common Soul) that should Endow it with those several Powers and Faculties. In short; why may not the Universe Really be Body and Soul, and every Particular Animal (as a part thereof) be Organ and Faculty, in the same sense that in our ordinary Common way of Conceiving, every Particular Animal is Body and Soul, and the Parts of it, Organs and Faculties?[15]

It should be explained that a faculty, to Burthogge, is a result of an organ in operation and a spirit that perceives the operation. That is, the eye as an organ does not see. It only operates so that the soul may see, using it as a medium. The result

14. Ibid., p. 156.
15. Ibid., pp. 237–38.

of the soul and the eye in conjunction is sight, but neither alone
could produce sight.[16] Also important to the way in which
Burthogge's system works is his distinction between a philosophical and popular definition of *soul*. The philosophical
definition makes the soul the sum total of all faculties. The
popular definition makes it a separate single consciousness that
is informed by the faculties but is not the faculties either singly
or in aggregate.

In fine, since nothing of Cogitation is done within us by the Soul
Immediately, but only by *means* of the *Understanding*, or of the will,
or of the sense, External, or Internal, and All these are rather Faculties
than Actions, I believe I have Reason to Conclude, that the Soul is
rather a System of the Faculties, or else a Principle of them, than that
it is a Perpetual never ceasing Exercise or Action. . . .[17]

The implications of the notion that God is the soul of the
world are as important as the idea itself. Burthogge's further
adaptations show what Pope must take into account for his
whole system in balancing God's presence as the soul of the
world. As an objection to his own system, Burthogge antici-
pates that it will seem to make God the immanent rather than
the transient cause of the world, and here he cites some biblical
passages, such as "in him we live, and move, and have our being," to show that God is immanent according to scripture.
Then he quotes Seneca, "What God is, in reference to the
World; that same the Soul is, in respect of a Man."[18] He also
gives a quotation from Marcus Aurelius and refers to the notes
in Thomas Gataker's edition of the *Meditations* (1652) for
proof of further support from the ancients. For Christian support he goes to Augustine and Origen.[19] Even with this im-
pressive array of supporters, Burthogge is still aware of the
danger of the position.

Only here it must be observed, that when *God* is compared unto a

16. Ibid., p. 239.
17. Ibid., p. 255.
18. Ibid., p. 257.
19. Ibid., pp. 258–59.

Soul, it must be understood with due limitation; to wit, as a Soul is taken only for a Principle of Powers and Actions, and not as it is an informing *Form,* or part of the Animal. . . .[20]

That is, Burthogge has already distinguished between a spirit that is pure spirit and one that works only through media. God is pure spirit and so is not by nature involved with media. Though he can inform media (and in the system being described does so) he is not limited to media as, for instance, the soul of man is, and he is not the result of their functioning. This distinction allows Burthogge to attribute to God the capacity to function as a soul according to the "popular definition" mentioned above, though he denies the validity of the popular definition when it is applied to the soul of man.

Burthogge also, and most importantly, deals with the objection that "*God* and *Nature* are confounded in his Hypothesis, so that it is not easie to say what is the interest of *God* in things, and what is *Natures,* or how they differ. . . ."[21] His answer is that there are second causes as well as first, and the differences between God's functioning and nature's are perhaps better explained by his hypothesis than any other.

For in *this,* God and Nature are distinguished, as the Soul of an Animal, and the System of Faculties; taking the Soul (as it is in the common Opinion) for the Principle of Faculties, and the Faculties for the immediate Principles of all actions of Animals.[22]

He also compares the difference between God's functioning and nature's to light. God would be, in this comparison, light, and the faculties of nature would be colors. Light, or God, is the primal causative impulse, and colors, or nature, are the operations of light in what can be perceived. Colors exist only in objects and are but modes of light. By this comparison Burthogge can free God of the responsibility for "the aberrations of Nature in Monsters," and he insists that the bungling of

20. Ibid., p. 259.
21. Ibid.
22. Ibid., p. 260.

second causes does not impeach the excellence of primary ones, just as "the scriblings of a bad mishaping Pen are not imparted to the hand that guides it." Still, with all this twisting in the toils of implication, Burthogge is not certain that the soul of the world is "God Himself" but takes it to be "the Mosaical Spirit." There is in Burthogge's whole discussion much that is not relevant to Pope's use of the idea that "All are but parts of one stupendous whole,/Whose body nature is, and God the soul," but he does make the issues clear, and he also gives an excellent indication of what elements such a description of the world's composition will add to a writer's systematic analysis of the relationship between the creator of the world and the existence of evil. This relationship is close to the one that was thought to exist between physical and moral evil.

Pope's purpose in making the assertion is, however, the key to the way in which the *Essay on Man* should be read, and this purpose is observable, for the reader, in what the statement accomplishes or attempts to accomplish. Pope is proclaiming the spirituality of the world and saying that it is not merely the product of intelligence and spirit but also contains them. God is present immediately rather than at a distance. As far as the relationship of body to soul that is applied here is concerned, Pope evidently had accepted for a number of years the sort of connection suggested by the passage under consideration. Earlier in his career, in the *Essay on Criticism*, he wrote that the functioning of art within a poem works in the same life-giving way in which the soul inhabits the body (ll. 76–79).

Of particular importance, however, is the way the word *soul* is being used in the passages from both poems. The informing soul that guides each motion and sustains every nerve is clearly a complex, not to say ambiguous, concept. Pope is apparently making use of the quite general notion that the soul (or purposeful guidance) functions in the world through three different manifestations. The rational soul, possessed by man alone, thinks and understands. The sensitive soul, found in man and brutes, is the principle of life, instinct, self-preservation. The vegetative soul, the only kind possessed by plants, is found in all life and brings about growth and the nutritive processes. Soul, therefore, existed with varying degrees of consciousness in its workings, but the working of all these kinds of soul was often regarded as a function of one comprehensive, purposive faculty. In fact the supposed relationship between the manifestations of soul are difficult to pin down, and probably the analogy to the total human being is intended by Pope primarily to suggest a kind of relationship rather than to give a one-to-one analogy. Numerous references in the *Essay* to heaven's forming and looking on at the world suggest that Pope did not intend to involve God so much in the world that he is not both apart from it and its maker. Burthogge's distinctions give some insight into important possibilities that should be included in any interpretation of Pope's analogy.

Pope's assertion should probably be observed as the solution to a singular problem rather than as gratuitous system-making, and his reliance on the age-old notion that man is a microcosm of the macrocosm gave him an opportunity to direct his whole system by conscious intention while leaving the parts to operate independently, effectively, and beyond the responsibility of the motivating consciousness of the entirety. In man the distinguishing function of reason is its ruling of the creature as a unit. To Pope this does not mean, as it might to others, that man is predominantly reasonable. He is distinguishing between single, partial, and momentary drives or needs in man and man as a unified and total creature that must have a single purpose as well as multitudinous partial purposes in order to survive and not be fractured into atoms. There will be occasion later to comment on his solution to man's apparent fragmentation. His solution to the fragmentation of the world is cut from the same cloth. There are countless individual phenomena each pulling in its own direction, but there is also a transcendent common purpose in the organic whole that these phenomena comprise, and the soul, which Pope says is God, rules the movement of the organism as a whole, though not every individual movement of every part.

Still, as Burthogge demonstrates, the solution is certain to be controversial because of what it does not do, despite what it may achieve. If God is there, inside, creating all the time, then what he creates, he is responsible for; and there are pain and suffering, not to mention monsters, in the world. Pope's solution to this ramification of his system is to be found in the other half of the assertion: Nature is the body of the world. In the same way that the body of man decays and dies but does not degrade the soul by doing so, the body of nature acts of itself. The body of nature contains the soul that is God and operates in harmony with it, but nature responds directly to the soul only as a unit while its parts grow and heal and decay by mute purposes of their own.

Now, these last three sentences are an interpretation and considerable extension of Pope's argument, for he literally says none of it. He does respond to the need stemming from this train of thought, even though he may have had a somewhat different chain of consequences in mind. With these connections between what occurs in the world and who is responsible for it, God as the soul of the world becomes entangled with the origin of evil. The purpose of Pope's entire poem is to account for the origin of evil, or at least the existence of evil, in such a way as to keep God's reputation intact. His special problem is to provide an explanation for the origin of evil that will vindicate God even though God is involved in the world as its soul.

A closer look at some issues in the controversies over the origin of evil will show more accurately where Pope stood among his contemporaries in their solutions to the problem. One of the more imposing attempts to solve the problem of the origin of evil was a text that has already been discussed in some detail, King's *Essay on the Origin of Evil*. When King wrote the original Latin version he was bishop of Derry, and later he became archbishop of Dublin. By the time Edmund Law's translation was published in 1730 (the title page says 1731) King was dead.[23] King's vindication of God is based on an a priori argument from God's attributes. He does not deny the existence of evil in the world but sets out to explain why it is there.

These Evils must be consider'd particularly, and we are to shew how they may be reconcil'd with the Government of an infinitely powerful and beneficent Author of Nature. For, since there is such a Being, 'tis ask'd, as we said before, Whence come Evils? Whence so many *Inconveniencies* in the Work of a most *good,* most *powerful God?* Whence that perpetual War between the very *Elements,* between *Animals,* between *Men?* Whence *Errors, Miseries* and *Vices,* the constant Companions of human Life from its Infancy? Whence Good to Evil Men, Evil to the Good? If we behold any thing irregular in the Works of Men, if any Machine answers not the End it was made for; if we find something in it repugnant to itself or others, we attribute that to the Ignorance, Impotence, or Malice of the Workman: but since these Qualities have no place in God, how come they to have place in any thing? Or, Why does God suffer his Works to be deform'd by them?[24]

Though King paints a dark picture of human life, he does insist that there is much more good than evil in nature, as shown by the fact that all creatures do whatever is in their power to maintain their existence.[25] Here in King's description there is the profitable reminder that he and Pope and many of their contemporaries are concerned with culpable evil and not with felt evil or even abstract evil. If, instead of a singular, abstract quality, evil is something for which blame is deserved, then that

23. King has been a popular candidate for a direct influence on Pope. The translation of the *Essay* by Edmund Law was not available until 1730, but the Latin version was published in 1702. In addition the pamphlet *A Key to Divinity: Or a Philosophical Essay on Free-Will* (London, 1715) is a translation other than Law's of the key sections of the *Essay*. It should be noted that the real crux of King's argument concerns these questions of free will and has little if anything to do with Pope's argument. The part that bears resemblance to Pope is neither original nor unusual.

24. King, pp. 73–74.

25. Ibid., p. 78.

which is unavoidable for some excellent reason cannot properly be called evil, no matter what abstract qualities it may have.

King divides existent evil into three kinds, evils of defect, natural evil, and moral evil. He defends the existence of each in a similar manner, but the three types are distinguishable. All created things must fall short of perfection because of the fact that God is perfection; if he were to create perfection he would recreate himself—an impossibility because God is self-existent. Since only God is self-existent, whatever else was created had to be created out of nothing, and what was thus created out of nothing must be infinitely short of perfection. Even though creatures must be imperfect, however, they can have much good in them; and were God to refuse to create them because of the evil which must result from their imperfection, he would have thereby to refuse to create the good of which they are capable as well. "Imperfection then arose from the Infinity of Divine Goodness. Had not God been infinitely Good, perhaps he might not have suffer'd imperfect Beings; but have been content in himself, and created nothing at all."[26] It is certain, however, that the amount of good in the creation is greater than the amount of evil, and it is certain that whatever is created is as good as it could have been, granting that God created a whole universe and that it is in relation to the functioning of the whole that the goodness or badness of parts is to be judged.

Now it is to be believ'd, that the present System of the World was the very best that could be, with regard to the Mind of God in framing it. It might have been better perhaps in some Particulars, but not without some new, and probably greater Inconveniencies, which must have spoil'd the Beauty, either of the whole, or of some chief Part.[27]

If we look at parts, considered singly, they will of course display the results of the necessary evil of imperfection, for "a Part must needs come short, both of the *Divine Perfection,* and the Per-

26. Ibid., p. 83.
27. Ibid., p. 84–85.

fection of the *whole*,"[28] but if we look at the whole instead, we cannot but see that it is justly the work of God, that there is no evil but what could have been prevented only by the introduction of a worse.

Natural evil, of course, shares the results of the necessary evil of imperfection, but it is more directly the result of the fact that the part of the universe we see is made out of matter and, being made of matter, is subject to the friction essential to matter. Matter, in order to be useful and to have life, must be put into motion, and there must be a contrariety of motion for the same reason. Therefore, the existence of matter and motion makes unavoidable the clashes and bumps which follow upon colliding matter. It is from this source that natural evil derives. The only thing that can be required is that there should be no more friction than is necessary, and, knowing God's attributes, "who but a very rash, indiscreet Person will affirm, that God has not actually made choice of this?"[29]

Behold now how Evils spring from and multiply upon each other, while infinite Goodness still urges the Deity to do the very best. This moved him to give *Existence* to Creatures which cannot exist without *Imperfections* and *Inequality*. This excited him to create *Matter* and to put it in *Motion,* which is necessarily attended with Separation and Dissolution, Generation and Corruption. This persuaded him to couple Souls with Bodies, and to give them mutual Affections, whence proceeded Pain and Sorrow, Hatred and Fear, with the rest of the Passions, yet all of them, as we have seen, are necessary.[30]

In reply to the charge that man, because of special qualities or special abilities to suffer, should have had some additional consideration in the whole plan, King refers to the fulness of the universe, a fulness with no room into which man could have been moved.[31] The idea is simpler than its proponents might

28. Ibid., p. 86.
29. Ibid., pp. 100–1.
30. Ibid., p. 116.
31. For Pope's use of this idea see the discussion of a necessarily full system in chapter 1.

sometimes make it sound. The real point is merely that since it is God's goodness which moved him to create at all, that goodness also moved him to create whatever good could be created; therefore, the world is not full of vacancies which might be filled with better advantage to the inhabitants than the places they now fill. Man exists because he is, by the standards of God's goodness, worthy of existence, just as everything else is. There is, therefore, no change of position available for him.[32]

Moral evil by definition stems from choices. If it is to be distinguished from the other kinds of evil, the definition of choice must be made clear. If the creature is naturally subject to imperfections of the will, then moral evil appears to be an evil of imperfection, and man is not responsible for it; therefore, moral evil is closely bound up with questions of free will, since, in order for moral evil to exist by King's definition, the choosing of morally evil actions must be by the creature. If the choice is not really a choice, if the creature is not genuinely responsible for it, nothing that can legitimately be called moral evil exists.

King discusses two prevalent theories of free will in order to make a distinction upon which his own ideas are based. One group of writers admits the existence of liberty from compulsion but not from internal necessity. If a being is free to put into action what it prefers, then it can be said to be free,[33] but this does not mean that it is free to prefer whatever it will, for objects have qualities. The qualities are either attractive or they are not, and the only consideration that determines the being's freedom of action is its ability to pursue what it finds attractive. It cannot, however, be free of what it is or what the world is.

In this view, the being who is to perform an act of willing has a certain set of characteristics, and the things to be chosen or rejected also have certain qualities. Goodness (or pleasure or whatever will finally determine choice) is an agreement of characteristics and qualities; what things are in themselves, there-

32. See the quotation from King above, pp. 34–35.
33. This distinction is also discussed above, pp. 21–26, 28–30.

fore, determines what will happen in the action of choosing. King's view of this theory is that it ends in what actually must be called necessity: "If it be granted that this is the Nature of our Elections, there's no doubt but all our Actions are really and truly necessary."[34] The additional conclusions which King says must be drawn from this view of the universe is that God works under the same restrictions and that, therefore, the whole universe is necessary.

Now, from this Hypothesis, which they extend to the Divine as well as Human Will, the following Corollaries seem deducible. First, that nothing in Nature could be done otherwise than it is. For, the whole Series of things being as it were connected together by Fate, there's no Room for Chance or Liberty, properly so call'd: *Contingency* then is removed out of Nature.[35]

The second theory of liberty claims for itself freedom from necessity as well as compulsion. It holds approximately the same views concerning the goodness of objects as related to existent appetites,[36] but it adds another dimension to the makeup of the individual. The individual moves largely under the rule of the duty he owes to God and to his society rather than under the rule of the mere animal appetites. Creatures other than man are moved by appetites and objects corresponding to them, but man is distinguished from these creatures because of a main principle that singles out some chief good against which other goods are measured and weighed. The other goods are, in this process, made subservient to the main principle. Man, in this view, cannot choose anything unless it comes to him under the appearance of good, but objects may be seen in different ways and may have different relationships to the chief good. With regard to any individual good, actual movement toward it may be suspended until a determination is made as to whether the chief good will be served or not. In other words, the individual adjusts and chooses among the objects

34. King, p. 154.
35. Ibid., p. 156.
36. Ibid., p. 161.

presented to his consciousness in order to make them conform to a central, large, and controlling interest.[37]

While King agrees that this point of view establishes a certain kind of liberty,[38] he has two strong objections to it. The first is that it depends on the notion that some things are naturally of such a character as to give pleasure to the acting being. Therefore, when the final view is taken, the individual's pleasure is the product of a natural relationship over which he has no control. Such immutable relationships and dependencies do not make the real and most important liberty possible. The second objection is an extension of the first. If immutable relationships exist between things, would not free will be a curse rather than a blessing? It would merely be the freedom to choose an evil rather than a good, a pain rather than a pleasure. If pleasures are derived from nature rather than one's own volition, then one would be better off if he were fated in every way so that he could not mistake his own happiness.

There is no need to deal at length with King's solution to this dilemma. Its primary attributes are noted above.[39] He posits, among other appetites and drives, a drive to the act of willing. He says that his observation of human beings in the world will not allow the view that they act and react within a system of prearranged relationships between objects and appetites. For one thing, many experiences are at first repugnant to the appetites but come through repeated encounters to be pleasurable. (His editor cites wines, tobacco, and olives as examples.) King suggests, with such observations in mind, that men can and do make things pleasurable by exercising on them the ability to choose, and finally he gives to God, who has no appetites to please, the characteristic of making things good by the act of choosing rather than being forced to choose those things which

37. This theory of motivation bears considerable similarity to Pope's theory of self-love as the dominant force of human nature as well as the predominant passion. King's resistance to it shows a significant difference between their schemes.
38. King, p. 166.
39. See chapter 1.

are naturally pleasing. Man shares this characteristic with God, and because man has this actual ability to choose, moral evil can exist. Then, of course, the question would be why man was given this attribute if from it such a scourge as moral evil was to arise. The primary answer to this objection is that there is room in the creation for free creatures and that free creatures are better than unfree ones because, by being free, they are nearer to God, who has freedom. In addition, King says that if creatures were to be able to react pleasurably only to those things which are naturally pleasurable to them, they would be the victims of their surroundings. If naturally pleasurable things happened along, men would find pleasure, but at best such pleasure could only be partial, and a man's happiness or a lack of it would depend largely, if not entirely, on chance. Therefore, a man's real happiness depends not on this ability merely to react pleasurably to those pleasurable things he luckily encounters, but rather on his ability to make those things he finds around him pleasurable by exercising upon them his primary faculty, the ability to obtain pleasure from choosing.

But if it be granted that things please us, not because the Understanding judges them to be eligible, but because we resolve to exercise our Free-Will in performing them, even these will become agreeable by Election, and the Understanding will perceive them to be made so, and not make them to be so. 'Tis not therefore the Office of the Understanding to govern the Will, but to discover means for the attainment of that which is chosen, and to give warning when it chooses such things as are absurd or impossible: For the Understanding, as we said before, judges that to be good which is agreeable to our Choice, except this lead us into Absurdities. In order therefore to avoid Absurdities, we make use of the Understanding as a Monitor, not a Master.[40]

This quotation emphasizes that King does not leave the field for choices completely free. Impossibilities and absurdities will not result in pleasure merely by being chosen. Certain relation-

40. King, p. 237.

ships between objects and affections cannot be denied—that is, they cannot be denied if they are present—but a being is not a slave to them; he merely must not ignore them, and his primary ability is to please himself. The distinction applies fully to both God and man. God is not determined to choose things by the qualities they have (such determination would make a thoroughly fated world), and man is not limited by the qualities of objects to his enjoyment of them, for such a limitation would deny him the responsibility for what he does. The source of moral evil, then, is this actual ability to choose, and moral evils are the result of using the ability wrongly. A wrong use would mean a use that ignores the realities of physical existence: some things are impossible, and others are unavoidably harmful. God allowed this state because (as with other kinds of evil) a worse would have resulted if he had not.

God could indeed cut off all Occasion of Sin, by taking away free Elections: But it is plain that this would be far from an Advantage to intelligent Agents. 'Tis our Business to prevent bad Elections, and if we will not, we suffer for our Folly: But God will procure the Good of the whole by our Folly no less than by our Wisdom.[41]

Another extended attempt to explain the origin of evil to God's credit is John Clarke's Boyle lectures of 1719 and 1720. John Clarke was Samuel Clarke's brother, and he shared some of Samuel's most characteristic ideas. He is, in his Boyle lectures, attempting to uphold the position that the creation is arbitrary and that, therefore, God was free in forming it. But he also holds that the differences between things are immutable. The two ideas were commonly held to be in conflict; however, John Clarke had the experience of his brother's correspondence with Leibniz before him, and he was unwilling to accept the extreme implication of Leibniz's necessity. Perhaps for this reason he does not argue that the world is the best but only that it is very good.

41. Ibid., pp. 280–81.

The evil of imperfection and natural evils Clarke explains by
the same argument that King uses.

But every Thing being subject to different *Laws* or *Rules;* this is the
Foundation of all those Inconveniencies complained of: And this was
not possible in the Nature of Things to be prevented: There could
have been no Degrees or Ranks of Creatures; there could have been
no Order or Harmony in the World, without such Differences. The
whole therefore is reduced to this, either that there must be no created Beings at all, or they must be liable to some *Evils* or other of
this Kind.⁴²

The existence of moral evil, however, depends upon the distinction King rejected.

For though it be true, that the Foundation of moral Virtue is laid in
the Nature and Reason of Persons and Things, is the necessary Result
of the different Relations and Proportions which they bear to each
other, when compared together, and consequently is eternal and
immutable; yet the Existence both of the *Persons* and the *Things*
themselves is arbitrary, and depends intirely upon the Will of the
Creator. The true Principle of religious Virtue therefore, is a con-
forming to the Circumstances and Relations of Persons and Things
upon this View, that *God* is the original Author of them; that, what
we call the Laws of Nature, are indeed the Rules prescribed by
Providence, under whose immediate Care and Inspection all Things
are; that every one of these is appointed for wise and good Ends;
and that therefore it is the Duty of intelligent and voluntary Agents,
to comply as much as is in their power, with what they thus find to
be the Will of God; and to promote, as far as they are able, what they
see to be his Design, in Obedience to his Will, in Expectation of be-
coming thereby acceptable to him, and capable of Reward from
him.⁴³

To King, it will be remembered, the system here summarized is
unacceptable because in it free will would do more harm than
good. King is on the verge of a controversy that will be dis-

42. John Clarke, "Origin of Evil," *BLS*, 3:196.
43. Ibid., "Moral Evil." *BLS*, 3:245.

cussed later concerning the source of moral obligation, but he represents a curiously dead-ended path on that road because of his concentration on free will. Freedom of will, as King describes it, seems to establish spirit as the basis of action, free from a necessary connection with the world's matter, but the connection he posits does not supply much insight into immediate motivation. His ingenious positing of a capacity for willing could easily be transmuted by a more worldly arguer into the principle of self-love, and with that change King would fit into the school of Daniel Waterland, John Clarke of Hull and others,[44] who are vehement (just as King is) against moral obligation from the reason of things because the reason of things is a yardstick available to all men independent of the authority of the established church.

Though there is much a priori reasoning in both King's and John Clarke's attempts to explain the origin of evil to God's advantage, both writers also attempt a posteriori justification of their conclusions. King justifies his power of election or free will by proving that man's real happiness is dependent on it; that is, man would genuinely be worse off without it. Then the fact that the capacity gets him into trouble is countered by the assurance that the trouble it gets him into is less than the trouble it gets him out of. Clarke, though he mentions the uselessness, or even perniciousness, of free will in a world of immutable relationships (he refers to it as the objection of the "ancient academicks"), finally makes moral evil an evil of defect.

But as Man is of a middle Nature, and partakes of the intellectual Powers and Faculties in common with the Angels, and also of the sensual Appetites and Desires in common with the Brute Creatures; He must under these Circumstances be perpetually *liable* to be imposed upon and deceived by the Objects of Sense, dictating Things different from the Objects of Reason.

And hence the Cause and Origin of every moral Evil, of the *actual*

44. In the present work reference is made to two John Clarkes. One, a schoolmaster and grammarian, is called John Clarke of Hull. The other, brother of Samuel Clarke and Boyle lecturer, is referred to by name alone.

Commission of so much Sin and Wickedness as we see practised in the World every Day, notwithstanding the Creator is infinitely wise and good; is very plain and evident. It is the *Abuse* of that *Liberty* which God Almighty has indued every Man with; which was intended for their Benefit and Perfection, and which they themselves pervert to their own Mischief and Ruin. That such *Liberty* is in itself an excellent Gift, must be acknowledged by every one, who thinks there is any Difference betwixt mere *Appetite* and *Reason,* betwixt an *Animal* and a *Rational* Life, and the Enjoyments and Happiness peculiar to each of them.[45]

The difference between King and Clark here may be relatively small, but it is, nevertheless, crucial. King admits that there are differences in things and that they must be observed, but these differences affect man only in extreme cases. Of course a man cannot stick his hand in a fire and choose not to be burned, but most human activity takes place well within such an extreme limit. Within the boundaries set up by physical danger, human beings are not dumbly guided by an affinity between a desire in a man and an object outside him that is suitable to the desire. King insists that to some considerable degree men give to objects the qualities they see in them, and because they do this they can make themselves at home in the world where the objects they encounter are accidentally present to them. Probably the clearest distinction between the operations described by King and Clarke is in the use of the understanding. To King the understanding does not discover the immutable relationships between things. It recognizes those things men can choose to enjoy, and it recognizes the outside limits within which choice can be made.[46] King gives to the understanding approximately the same function that Pope gives to reason, though Pope's coupling of reason with self-love and King's coupling of understanding with will are not close, since will is a mode of thought while self-love is the totality of the passions, or the drive of which the passions are modes. King's

45. John Clarke, "Moral Evil," *BLS,* 3:249.
46. See the quotation from King above, p. 63.

principle distinction gives to men a passion for willing, and he is thus able to combine will and passion at a crucial point.

The arguments of King and John Clarke give a clear indication of the issues that clustered around attempts to explain the evils, either real or apparent, perceived to be in the creation. The problem is quite clearly not merely to explain the evils but to explain them in such a way as to preserve God's free will and avoid assigning the working of the world to fate. Pope is apparently not concerned with the dangers of either concept. His assertion that the best possible world is a result of God's wisdom leads, quite explicitly in his system, to an unavoidable creation, and the lack of concern over free will manifested by this solution is again shown in his disposition of the origin of evil.

King reflects the general attitude that moral evil cannot be an evil of defect similar to natural evil, or man will lose the responsibility for it, and God will be to blame. John Clarke is willing to forego King's concern over these consequences and rest in the assurance that the liberty he describes is good even though it might be said to introduce moral evil. Pope does not even bother with the implication. He dismisses the problem as soluble by logical consistency. Natural evil and moral evil need not be explained differently. His antagonist, who believes that the world operates by general laws and that nothing was created perfect is guilty of shocking pride in his arrogant conclusion: "My foot-stool earth, my canopy the skies." Pope engages him in a dialectic.

> But errs not Nature from this gracious end,
> From burning suns when livid deaths descend,
> When earthquakes swallow, or when tempests sweep
> Towns to one grave, whole nations to the deep?
> "No ('tis reply'd) the first Almighty Cause
> "Acts not by partial, but by gen'ral laws;
> "Th' exceptions few; some change since all began,
> "And what created perfect?"—Why then Man?
> If the great end be human Happiness,

Then Nature deviates; and can Man do less?
As much that end a constant course requires
Of show'rs and sun-shine, as of Man's desires;
As much eternal springs and cloudless skies,
As Men for ever temp'rate, calm, and wise.
If plagues or earthquakes break not Heav'n's design,
Why then a Borgia, or a Catiline?
Who knows but he, whose hand the light'ning forms,
Who heaves old Ocean, and who wings the storms,
Pours fierce Ambition in a Caesar's mind,
Or turns young Ammon loose to scourge mankind?
From pride, from pride, our very reas'ning springs;
Account for moral as for nat'ral things:
Why charge we Heav'n in those, in these acquit?
In both, to reason right is to submit.

                                                    (I, 140–64)

Although the argument in this passage begins with a refutation of the idea that the world was made for man, the real subject is whether man's capability of commiting evil is a special
case in the full consideration of the origin of evil. The prideful
man is ready to admit that natural evil is not to be blamed on
God but is a result of the general working of the universe and
the fact that nothing is created perfect. This is, of course, the
idea expounded by both King and Clarke, and Pope apparently
accepts it since he lets it pass. He insists, however, that moral
evil should be accounted for in the same way. With his admission that only God really knows, he seems to be saying that if
men speculate on these matters at all, then they should be consistent in the sort of logic they apply. He states rather strongly
that men are wrong to assume that moral evil presents a special
case unsolvable by the same reason that accounts for natural
evil. The real source of error is in the initial assumption—that
man is the creature around whom the creation turns and for
whom it was formed:

Ask for what end the heav'nly bodies shine,
Earth for whose use? Pride answers, " 'Tis for mine:

> "For me kind Nature wakes her genial pow'r,
> "Suckles each herb, and spreads out ev'ry flow'r;
> "Annual for me, the grape, the rose renew
> "The juice nectareous, and the balmy dew;
> "For me, the mine a thousand treasures brings;
> "For me, health gushes from a thousand springs;
> "Seas roll to waft me, suns to light me rise;
> "My foot-stool earth, my canopy the skies."
>
> (I, 131–40)

In final comparison, then, Pope's argument is somewhat closer to Clarke's than to King's since Pope and Clarke give to moral evil the same origin as the evil of defect. Clarke, however, with his insistence on the arbitrariness of the creation, takes as one of his central points a view denied by Pope when he asserts that infinite wisdom must form the best of all possible worlds. All three writers agree (the notion seems nearly universal at the time) that natural evil or the evil of defect is inherent in the nature of created beings, and all agree that moral evil is the product of man's will. It is only at the hub of the issue that they disagree, and the issue demonstrates that, although they make some of the same assertions, the assumptions behind them and the ramifications from them differ sharply.

To return now to the original thread of the discourse, Pope's assertion that God is the soul of the world involves him in this matter of the origin of evil in a new way. King and Leibniz and John Clarke assume that the world is a creation and that God is its creator, but Pope's inclusion of God within the world as its soul involves God not only in what he has made but also in what he constantly continues to make by his immanence. Those writers who, like the Cambridge Platonists, are particularly committed to the immanent spirituality of the world frequently find it necessary to acquit God of the responsibility for the origin of evil in a manner different from that of King and Clarke because of the way they involve God in the world. Pope is involved with the same problem, and his solution is that of Cudworth and his followers. At the end of the first epistle Pope does say that "All partial evil [is] universal Good," but in the fourth epistle he returns to the subject.

> What makes all physical or moral ill?
> There deviates Nature, and here wanders Will.
> God sends not ill; if rightly understood,
> Or partial Ill is universal Good,
> Or Change admits, or Nature lets it fall,
> Short and but rare, 'till Man improv'd it all.
>
> (IV, 111–16)

The statement here is that all of the physical ill in the world is the result of deviations of nature; while all moral ill is the result of man's wandering will. This fits King and Clarke, but King and Pope differ on the source of these wanderings of the will. King attributes them to the existence of a positively desirable attribute, not to a necessary limitation in a necessarily (but rightly) limited creature. Then, however, Pope goes on to explain the existence of physical evil more thoroughly. Partial ill is of three kinds. (1) Some of it is universal good; what seems ill from a partial view is actually positively good in contributing to the whole. (2) Some of it is the product of change; that is, as King and Clarke also perceive, the material system in order to be alive must be a flux, and flux unavoidably admits destruction and dissolution. (3) Nature allows a third kind, and it is here that Pope introduces an idea that frees God, as soul of the world, from responsibility for what happens in the world. The evil that is the result of the world's malfunctioning he assigns to nature, or plastic nature, acting in the same manner as a vegetative or perhaps sensitive soul, having its own role to play in the functioning of parts, though unconcerned with and unaware of the movements of the whole. Therefore, as the whole analogy is observed, God is no more to blame for malfunctioning parts of the body of nature than a man's soul is responsible for an ingrown toenail. A man is responsible only for seeing that the ingrown toenail treads the straight and narrow, and God is responsible only for seeing that the whole creation gets where it is going.

Pope's assignment of some of natural evil to plastic nature is similar to the reasoning of Cudworth, Burthogge, and John Ray, scientist and fellow of the Royal Society. In Ray's very popular *The Wisdom of God Manifested in the Works of the Creation* he comes to the question of the manner in which the creation is kept going, and he cannot accept the notion that God set it going sometime in the past and that it then continued to work by the effect of the first motion.

Therefore there must, besides Matter and Law, be some Efficient, and that either a Quality or Power inherent in the Matter it self, which is hard to conceive, or some external intelligent Agent, either God himself immediately, or some *Plastick Nature.* This latter I incline to, for the Reasons alleg'd by Dr. Cudworth. . . .[47]

The reasons for rejecting the notion that God himself keeps the creation going are that such an arrangement would "render the Divine Providence operose, sollicitous and distractious." He says that if God were in constant action, the slow and methodical way in which things actually occur in the world would be "vain and idle Pomp or trifling Formality," and, lastly, he notices that "Errors and Bungles" occur in the world, and they suggest that the agent is not irresistible.

. . . Nature is such a thing as is not altogether uncapable, as well as Human Art, of being sometimes frustrated and disappointed by the indisposition of the Matter: Whereas an Omnipotent Agent would always do its Work infallibly and irresistibly, no ineptitude or stubbornness of the Matter being ever able to hinder such an one, or make him bungle or fumble in any thing.[48]

Ray subscribes to these ideas of Cudworth's because, though he would prefer to leave such matters to the vegetative power of the souls of individual plants and other creatures, there are objections of too great weight: "I therefore incline to Dr. *Cudworth's* Opinion, that God uses for these Effects the sub-

47. John Ray, *The Wisdom of God Manifested in the Works of the Creation,* 3d ed. (London, 1701), p. 54. See also Cudworth, pp. 147–50.
48. Ray, pp. 55–56.

ordinate Ministry of some inferiour *Plastick Nature;* as in his Works of Providence he doth of Angels."[49] Because of the bungling of nature in operation (some kinds of physical evils) Ray cannot accept the idea that God is himself working through the world, and he gives the blame (as Pope does) to nature. Furthermore this nature is personified into a force with a ministry to perform. To both of them, the origin of one kind of evil is the deviation of a necessarily imperfect administrator and not God directly, and both attempt to vindicate God by this line of reasoning.

The three ideas joined together in this chapter are not joined by Pope to form a single or connected argument, but he does include them and thereby demonstrates his awareness of certain relationships that were vital issues to his contemporaries, whether or not he was aware of them specifically as issues. The present study does not concern itself with sources, however, and the sole intention of the comparisons included here is to show against a background of contemporary thought how Pope managed his ideas. His juggling of the two themes of God as the soul of the world and plastic nature as the origin of the evil of malfunctioning in the world answers questions in a highly complex and involved argument. If the lack of immanent spirit in the world was no drawback, then the evils of the world were quite satisfactorily explained away as the necessary workings of an admirable machine, though the actual proponents of this explanation did not themselves exclude immanent spirit. Pope took the advantage of comparing the world to a man whose soul has no responsibility for the vegetative or digestive functions of the body while it moves the whole from place to place. But Boyle and Newton knew all these arguments, and they insisted that the soul is not the creator of the body; therefore, there is no analogy. Evidently one had to choose between what he wanted to gain and what he was willing to lose. There was no having everything.

49. Ibid., p. 56.

4

The Place of Reason

In his insistence that moral and physical evil should be accounted for in the same way, Pope gives one specific demonstration of a point that he reiterates throughout the *Essay on Man*. Man is not a special creature, apart from the fabric of the creation, for whose benefit the entire system was constructed. He is merely a part of the whole and occupies a place and plays a role just as other creatures do. In his specific analysis of man Pope continues to emphasize this central theme. Of primary significance is his evaluation of man's reason.

It should be noted that Pope does not prove or

attempt to prove that such a creature as man, with the exact characteristics possessed by man, would be abstractly necessary to any possible and excellent system. The necessity for man to exist in the present system stems from the requirement that the system be full if it is to cohere, and this is largely an a priori assertion. Given the mechanical necessity of man's existence, however, Pope shows two concerns: (1) What is, in fact, man's nature and (2) can that nature be justified by observation? The first of these concerns appears to come largely if not entirely from a controversy of long standing over whether man is predominantly a reasonable creature or primarily a self-loving, passionate creature.

Pope's most radical assertion in this area is that man is predominantly a creature of passion, not reason. In the contemporary context this assertion itself (calling up the spirits of Hobbes, Bernard Mandeville, and François La Rochefoucauld) might easily constitute an indictment of the creation, but Pope defends the creation by showing that passion or self-love *must* be the stronger motivating element in such a creature as man. Reason, by nature reflective and inactive, could not itself prompt matter into motion.

> Self-love, the spring of motion, acts the soul;
> Reason's comparing balance rules the whole.
> Man, but for that, no action could attend,
> And, but for this, were active to no end;
> Fix'd like a plant on his peculiar spot,
> To draw nutrition, propagate, and rot;
> Or, meteor-like, flame lawless thro' the void,
> Destroying others, by himself destroy'd.
> Most strength the moving principle requires;
> Active its task, it prompts, impels, inspires.
> Sedate and quiet the comparing lies,
> Form'd but to check, delib'rate, and advise.
> Self-love still stronger, as its objects nigh;
> Reason's at distance, and in prospect lie:
> That sees immediate good by present sense;
> Reason, the future and the consequence.

> Thicker than arguments, temptations throng,
> At best more watchful this, but that more strong.
> The action of the stronger to suspend
> Reason still use, to Reason still attend . . .
>
> (II, 59–78)

The question is not, then, whether man would not have filled his necessary link in the chain of being better if he had been predominantly reasonable. The chain demands what he is, and he is self-loving. A later chapter will deal with Pope's assurance that man's self-loving nature produces the proper moral effects, as well as the proper mechanical ones.

Although the assertion that reason is weaker than self-love is far more important than any of Pope's other individual conclusions about reason, it is supported by those individual conclusions; therefore, those conclusions are of interest to the reader because they form the foundation for the controversial assertion that reason is weaker than self-love. Pope's assertions about reason come from his intention to show that man is appropriate to his "state and place," that he is a functioning part of a massive system. Here, as usual, there is no question of the abstract perfection of man's reason, but only the relative soundness of the combination of mental capacities that exists. To be sure, in the contemporary context Pope's demotion of reason to second in command might easily be taken as an attack on reason and the creature who possesses it in the degree described. It was often taken for granted that reason should be man's predominant characteristic, that man is the *animal rationale*. But Pope never attacks reason itself in the poem. In order to humble man's pride he stresses the limitations of human reason, and to vindicate God he shows that man's reason, however limited, is what the system demands.

Early in the first epistle Pope begins an assessment of reason that is modest and conservative, for clearly he is engaged in a train of thought that is familiar to readers of the *Essay on Criticism*—man is in greater danger of overreaching than of falling short. Man's greatest need is for restraint and discipline, not inspiration or encouragement. In order to emphasize this train of thought Pope stresses the limitations of reason, especially as it attempts to deal with large and comprehensive problems.

> Say first, of God above, or Man below,
> What can we reason, but from what we know?
>
> (I, 17–18)

The simple assertion that we can reason only from what we know is a thoroughgoing commonplace, but even though no one would be much inclined to dispute the point, its meaning is clear only in a context where "what we know" is defined. Pope phrases the question so as to impose a limitation on man's capacities rather than recommend a method by which man can soar to new heights of brilliance, but the couplet quoted has suggested to some readers that in limiting man's reasoning to some process following only from what we know, Pope was recommending what the age called analogical reasoning.

Basic to analogical reasoning was the principle that the universe is a uniform fabric and that, as a consequence, one can know something about the whole, or about other parts, by examining whatever parts are available. One can, therefore, learn a great deal about the universe or about God, though one obviously cannot see them whole, by examining the immediate world and drawing analogies from it. This basic notion of analogy is exemplified by George Cheyne, physician and fellow of the Royal Society.

All the *Integral* Parts of *Nature*, have a beautiful *Resemblance, Similitude,* and *Analogy* to one another, and to their Almighty *Original,* whose Images, more or less expressive according to their several Orders and Gradations, in the *Scale* of Beings, they are; and they who are Masters in the noble Art of just *Analogy,* may from a tolerable Knowledge in any one of the *Integral* Parts of Nature, extend their Contemplations more securely to the whole or any other *Integral* Part less known.[1]

1. George Cheyne, *Philosophical Principles of Religion,* 2d ed. (London, 1715), p. 5.

Cheyne here states the principle (common to all varieties of analogical reasoning) that similarities can be assumed between what is seen and what is unseen, and, thereby, knowledge of the unseen can be satisfactorily projected. The general principle might be adapted in making descriptive statements about God, as it was by Thomas Burnett, Boyle lecturer in 1724.

. . . We must observe, that, as there is nothing future to God, but all things are eternally present to him; so those affections, that arise from the good, or evil, consider'd as future, such as hope, desire, or fear, cannot be ascrib'd to him, any otherwise, than in condescension to our Weakness; and they must be always understood, as spoken after the manner of Men:

But as for such of them, as relate to a present good, or evil, such as delight and joy, grief or anger; there is doubtless something in the Divine Nature, as I said, analogous to these operations in us, tho' altogether without our imperfections. . . .[2]

But an analogical process of this sort was controversial because it implied limitations unsatisfactory to two extreme points of view. It implied, on the one side, that since God and man are similar we can account for God's actions and motivations by human capacities. Burnett's final qualification is in harmony with this objection. The kind of anthropomorphizing Burnett works to avoid could lead to the hottest of issues: If we can know God in this way, what is the need of revelation? From the other extreme, the need to reason analogically could also form the basis of a more skeptical frame of mind. A writer might assert that human beings are so far from real truth that they can know only by analogy. Since God differs from men not only in degree but in kind as well, there is no way for man to know God as he is, any more, as William King puts it, than for a blind man to know the properties of light. The dangers of this point of view, especially to the rationalist divines and the deists, is that it puts God beyond the ken of man and erases all certainty from religion. The advantage of the approach is

2. *BLS*, 3:420.

that it increases the need for revelation by its reliance on mysterious awareness.

A different sort of analogy gives at least a ray of light. Functional analogy allows one to have the cake of mystery but eat the frosting of certainty. It is based on a similarity of needs and functions rather than characteristics and operations. In order for man to make those things he manipulates do what he wants them to do, in order to produce those effects he wants to produce, he uses his understanding. God also manipulates things and makes them produce one set of effects rather than another. One might say, therefore, that God uses his understanding to achieve what he desires to achieve. But if man wished to comprehend God's understanding, he could not do so, for it is in both degree and kind beyond him. He could, however, see that God had an attribute which enabled him to produce those effects he preferred. That attribute would be analogous to man's reason or understanding because both fulfill the same function in a complex operating being. This would not mean, however, that God thinks as man thinks or that God's view of man's understanding and his own would have any similarity except that they serve the same relative purpose. There is, in this modification, not an analogy between what things are, but rather between what they do, what purpose they serve.

These two different ways of talking about analogy are the same in their assumption that an analogy exists between the known and the unknown. They differ primarily in the following. One assumes that through analogy truth has been described. The other assumes that through analogy the existence of an analogy has been established, but all that can be known is that the analogy is a true one. The actual qualities of the unknown half of the analogy cannot be apprehended. All that can be known is that analogies exist between parts because of the functions they fulfill.

This second attitude toward analogy is well exemplified by Peter Browne, bishop of Cork. In the first place, Browne admits the validity and necessity of analogical reasoning.

But since there can be no *Perfection* in the Creature, any otherwise than as it bears *Some* Resemblance or Similitude of him, who is the Fountain of it all; then all *Intelligent* Creatures especialy must be more or less perfect, as they bear a greater or less Semblance and *Analogy* with his infinite incomprehensible Perfections: And consequently all their Notions and *Conceptions* of the Divine Being must be more or less sublime, exalted, and exact; in Proportion to that Resemblance which their *Own* essential Perfections bear to his, who is the *Standard* of all Perfection.[3]

Browne advocates this position in a system based largely on the principle that "our five *Senses* . . . are . . . the only *Source* and Inlets of those Ideas, which are the intire *Groundwork* of all our Knowledge both *Human* and *Divine*,"[4] and he attempts to discover what information is available to human capacities thus limited.

No, *Divine* Information gives us no *New* Faculties of Perception, but is adapted to those we *Already have;* nor doth it exhibit to the *Immediate* View of the Intellect *Any,* the *Least glimmering* Idea of things purely spiritual, intirely abstracted from all *Sensation* or any Dependence upon it: But it is altogether performed by the *Intervention* and Use of those Ideas which are *Already* in the Mind; first conveyed to the Imagination from the Impression of external Objects upon the Organs of *Sensation;* then variously *Alter'd* and diversify'd by the Intellect; and afterwards by its Operations of *Judgment* and *Illation,* wrought up into an endless Variety of *Complex Notions* and *Conceptions;* which takes in the whole Compass of our merely temporal and *Secular* Knowledge. Now, all this is transfer'd from *Earth* to *Heaven,* by way of *Semblance* and *Analogy:* So that the *Ideas* simple and compound; the *Complex Notions* and *Conceptions;* the *Thoughts* and *Reasonings;* the *Sentiments* and *Apprehensions;* the *Imaginations,* and *Passions,* and *Affections* of an *Human* Mind; together with the *Language* and *Terms* by which we express them, become *Subservient* to all the real Ends and Purposes of *Revelation.*[5]

3. Peter Browne, *The Procedure, Extent, and Limits of Human Understanding* (London, 1728), p. 456.

4. Ibid., p. 55.

5. Ibid., pp. 473–74.

The process of analogical reasoning in this way is not a bad tool so long as its limitations are realized and the conclusions reached through the process are recognized as unreal but operationally necessary.

NOTHING is more evident, than that we have no *Idea* of God, as he is in himself; and it is for want of such an Idea, that we frame to ourselves the most excellent *Conception* of him we can, by putting together into one, the greatest Perfections we observe in the Creatures, and particularly in our own reasonable Nature, to stand for his Perfections. Not most grosly arguing and inferring, that God is (in Effect and Consequence) such an one as our selves, only infinitely enlarged and *Improved* in all our natural Powers and Faculties; but concluding, That our greatest Excellencies are the best, and aptest, and most correspondent *Representations* only of his incomprehensible Perfections; which infinitely transcend the most exalted of what are in any *Created* Beings, and are far above out of the reach of all human Imagination.[6]

Browne regards the result of analogical reasoning as valid. He distinguishes this type of reasoning from metaphorical, in which the objects have no actual similarity. Browne's point is that to know God in this way is to know him as he really is, not as he is in essence but as he is in terms of relationships that human beings can comprehend.

The necessity to accommodate mysterious concepts to the limitations of human experience was also useful for scriptural interpretation. It freed an interpreter from the literal wording and allowed an appeal to the spirit of the text. Nothing could be clearer than the Bible's adaptation of its assertions to the minds and conceptual vocabularies of men. God is spoken of as having both limbs and organs not because God has such appendages but because the human ability to perceive is capable of no other terminology.[7]

Pope, however, is rather suspicious of reasoning by analogy.

He, who thro' vast immensity can pierce,

6. Ibid., pp. 85–86.

7. Burnett, quoted above (p. 78), uses this approach.

> See worlds on worlds compose one universe,
> Observe how system into system runs,
> What other planets circle other suns,
> What vary'd being peoples ev'ry star,
> May tell why Heav'n has made us as we are.
> But of this frame the bearings, and the ties,
> The strong connections, nice dependencies,
> Gradations just, has thy pervading soul
> Look'd thro'? or can a part contain the whole?
>
> (I, 23–32)

Perhaps he is not entirely consistent with his principle, but he explicitly limits our knowledge of God to the world and scoffs at system-making that goes beyond the evidence of immediate experience. To be told that man can reason only from what he knows, then, is not of much help to one attempting to discover man's limitations, unless he is also told what man knows and how he comes to know it.

The French Cartesian, Nicholas Malebranche, for example, expounds on the evils and dangers of the combination of the senses and liberty (the latter serving much the same offices Pope assigns to reason), but he argues that we can reason only from what we know.

> Neither must we puzzle our Heads with enquiring whether there are in the Bodies about us some other Qualities, besides those of which we have clear Ideas; for we must only reason upon our Ideas; and if there be any thing of which we have no clear, distinct and particular Idea, we shall never know it, nor argue from it with any Certainty: Whereas, perhaps, by reasoning upon our Ideas, we may follow Nature, and perhaps discover that she is not so hidden as is commonly imagin'd.[8]

However, within Malebranche's whole system, what we know is ideas from which we cannot withhold assent without an inner reproof, and these ideas are communications from God, which the understanding receives passively: "The Understand-

8. Nicholas Malebranche, *Treatise Concerning the Search after Truth*, trans. T. Taylor, 2d ed. (London, 1700), 2:73.

ing acts not at all, but only receives Light, or the Ideas of Things, through its necessary Union with Him who comprehends all beings in an intelligible manner. . . ."[9]

On the other hand, to Peter Browne, who also argues that we must reason from what we know, what we know is "outward appearances and sensible effects," and he argues that we do not need to know more (adding his kind of analogical reasoning to this base).

. . . we are intirely in the dark as to the inward Structure and Composition of the minute Particles of all Bodies; and can with no degree of Certainty judge or determine any thing concerning them, but from their outward Appearances and sensible Effects. . . . And if we had Sagacity and Acuteness of Sense enough to penetrate into the very *Intimate Essences* of Things, and into the exact Configuration of the *Minutest* Parts of Matter, it would perhaps answer no other end but that of useless Speculation and Amusement.[10]

Browne consistently commits himself to the position that our only source of ideas is the senses (though reason has a capacity for rearranging and modifying the sensations).[11] Browne and Malebranche present two extremes, but reasoning from what we know still represents no very clear limitation, because from the wide variety of uses even within those extremes the content of what men are supposed to know was subject to a confusing variety of assumption or interpretation.[12]

9. Ibid., p. 106.

10. Browne, pp. 209–10.

11. See above, pp. 80–81.

12. For example, the following: *"We ought only to Reason upon such things, whereof we have clear and distinct Ideas; and by a necessary consequence, we must still begin with the most simple and easie Subjects, and insist long upon them, before we undertake the Enquiry into such as are more composed and difficult"* (Malebranche, *Search After Truth,* 2:50). Referring to Malebranche: *"That we ought not to Reason but only of those things whereof we have clear Ideas. . . ."* (John Norris, *Reflections upon the Conduct of Human Life,* 2d ed. [London, 1691], p. 83). *"It is plain we know not the* Essences *of Things by* Intuition; *but can only reason about them, from what we know of their different* Properties *or* Attributes" (Samuel Clarke, "A Discourse Concerning the Unchangeable Obligations of Natural Religion, and the Truth and Certainty of the Christian Revelation," *BLS,*

Beyond this too general restriction to "what we know," Pope's restrictions on reason stem largely from two sources, though the dividing line between them is not always readily apparent. Part of the time man is exhorted to restrain himself within clear limits because he cannot go beyond them anyway. Part of the time restraint is recommended because even if man were to go beyond self-imposed limits he would gain no palpable reward by doing so. Though at times the argument may sound as if man actually threatens the structure of the creation by his striving, no stretch of the imagination can suggest the actuality of such a threat. The issue must be man's peace of mind. Man is counseled to restrain himself within just boundaries for three reasons: (1) these boundaries are natural and he cannot go beyond them; (2) they would be of no practical value to him if he were able to surpass them; (3) his real happiness lies within them.

If Pope's limitation of man's reasoning material to "what we know" is, by itself, no very clear guide, the reader may want to discover more precisely what Pope thinks the boundaries of human knowledge to be.

II:61). "That we have no Idea of Matter, abstracted from all its Attributes and sensible Qualities, *i.e.* from all the Ideas we have of it, is very sure, nor is it easy to conceive how we should; but then I say that 'tis impossible to argue and reason about it, impossible to draw any Consequences from it, farther than our Ideas go" (Thomas Morgan, *Enthusiasm in Distress:* or, *An Examination of the* Reflections upon Reason [London, 1722], pp. 24–25). "For no doubt our *Simple* Ideas and their *Compounds* must be supposed *Known,* before we attempt any *Farther* Knowledge by *Inference....*" (Browne, p. 426). "Now, I conceive, it is much safer and more reasonable to argue from known Fact to What is really fit and right for God to do, than to endeavour the Overthrow of What is certain Fact, by uncertain Presumptions what the Divine Attributes require" (John Conybeare, *A Defense of Reveal'd Religion* [London, 1732], p. 107). (While this quotation from Conybeare is rather far from Pope's text it is extremely apt. A frequent answer to those who attempted to judge what God ought to do was, as in this quotation, that the best guide for what God ought to do is what he has done.) "By the help of truths already known more may be discovered" (William Wollaston, *The Religion of Nature Delineated,* 7th ed. [London, 1750], p. 73).

Say first, of God above, or Man below,
What can we reason, but from what we know?
Of Man what see we, but his station here,
From which to reason, or to which refer?
Thro' worlds unnumber'd tho' the God be known,
'Tis ours to trace him only in our own.

(I, 17–22)

This quotation appears to limit what we know to what is available to our direct perception; of particular importance, we cannot know what is too big for us to see. Man cannot fathom God because a part cannot contain the whole of which it is a part. But to Pope and his contemporaries, in large number, this geometrical observation did not make knowledge of the world so hopeless of attainment as the attempt to make a geometrical part contain its whole would be for a geometrician. The writers who use the argument, and it was quite commonplace, do not usually find themselves at a loss for extensive knowledge of God. The argument characteristically leaves open an area for retreat to faith or submission. Many of Pope's contemporaries were able to argue with considerable assurance on a priori grounds and still seek shelter in comprehensive ignorance, should a conflicting piece of evidence arise. The combination of faith and reason made such difficulties inevitable when an exclusive reliance on either presumably would not have.[13]

13. In addition to Mack's quotations from Dryden and Pascal, see the following: ". . . Human Reason in its largest Capacity and Extent . . . is after all but a *Finite* thing . . . since 'tis impossible that what has Bounds should be able totally and adequately to Comprehend what has None, or that *Finite* should be the Measure of *Infinite*" (John Norris, *An Account of Reason and Faith: In Relation to the Mysteries of Christianity* [London, 1697], p. 177). ". . . It is impossible the *lesser* should contain and comprehend the *greater* . . ." (John Harris, "Eight Sermons," *BLS*, 1:371). "To doubt whether his *Nature,* and *manner* of Existence may be in reality thus *incomprehensible* to us, is to doubt whether the *less* may not contain the *greater* . . ." (Law in King, p. 47n). "As our minds are *finite,* they cannot without a contradiction comprehend what is *infinite.* And if they were inlarged to ever so great a capacity, yet so long as they retain their general nature, and continue to be of the *same kind,* they would by that be only renderd able to apprehend *more* and *more finite* ideas; out of which,

What these limitations on reason, expressed in broad and general terms, seem to push toward is a limitation of human knowledge to sense experience. Locke had apparently carried the field with his assertion that the senses set up the boundaries of human knowledge, but the idea was common before the publication of the *Essay Concerning Human Understanding*. Pope's limitation of knowledge to what can be seen in our world has the effect of denying that ingenious human speculation can be the foundation of certainty. Human beings know little because the material for knowing much is not available to them, and only their pride makes them think they know more. Pope does limit knowledge to the senses. He scoffs at the Platonists for going beyond the senses.

> Go, soar with Plato to th' empyreal sphere,
> To the first good, first perfect, and first fair;
> Or tread the mazy round his follow'rs trod,
> And quitting sense call imitating God. . . .
>
> (II, 23–26)

---

howsoever increased or exalted, no positive idea of the *perfection* of God can ever be formed. For a *Perfect* being must be *infinite,* and perfectly *One:* and in such a nature there can be nothing *finite,* nor any *composition* of finites" (Wollaston, p. 168).

For a summary of Pope's entire position, though a less close parallel in words, the following quotation from Samuel Clarke is interesting: "For as, in a great *Machine,* contrived by the Skill of a consummate Artificer, fitted up and adjusted with all conceivable Accuracy for some very difficult and deep-projected Design, and polished and fine-wrought in every part of it with Admirable Nicety and Dexterity; any Man, who saw and examined one or two Wheels thereof, could not fail to observe in those single Parts of it, the admirable Art and exact Skill of the Workman; and yet the Excellency of the End or Use for which the Whole was contrived, he would not at all be able, even tho' he was himself a skilful Artificer, to discover and comprehend, without seeing the Whole fitted up and put together: So tho' in every part of the *natural* World, considered even single and unconnected, the Wisdom of the great Creator sufficiently appears; yet his Wisdom, and Justice, and Goodness in the Disposition and Government of the *moral* World, which necessarily depends on the Connexion and Issue of the whole Scheme, cannot perhaps be distinctly and fully comprehended by any Finite and Created Beings, much less by frail, and weak, and short-lived Mortals, before the Period and Accomplishment of certain great Revolutions" ("Discourse," *BLS,* 2:116).

To be sure *sense* in this passage is ambiguous, but one of its meanings must be *the senses*. A few lines later, when Pope attacks those who regard the passions (or self-love) as conflicting, he asserts the interdependence of sense and reason.

> Let subtle schoolmen teach these friends to fight,
> More studious to divide than to unite,
> And Grace and Virtue, Sense and Reason split,
> With all the rash dexterity of Wit:
> Wits, just like fools, at war about a Name,
> Have full as oft no meaning, or the same.
>
> (II, 81–86)

With the senses as the boundaries of "what we know" the reader is somewhat closer to the crux of Pope's analysis of reason, but Pope gives further clarification of how we know what we know by describing certain guides which reason has available to it within the whole system. These guides are part of the system and mirror the design of its working. For reason does not act independently of experience. Pope tells reason to observe the operation of the world in order to be enlightened. Because of the difficulty of knowing the whole (and certainty about anything would demand such knowledge) Pope prescribes a self-imposed drawing-in of man's speculations to man himself and away from the world at large. Man's primary active concern is with himself, though his primary passive and submissive concern may be with God.

> The bliss of Man (could Pride that blessing find)
> Is not to act or think beyond mankind. . . .
>
> (I, 189–90)

Actually there are two ideas at work in this line of reasoning. First there is the observed weakness and limitation of man's knowledge, accompanied by the realization that imagination and complicated ratiocination can make man think that he has considerably extended the boundaries of what he knows. But part of what man is, is this capacity to deceive himself. The capacity is harmful only when prideful self-assessment leads man to conclude that what he imagines himself to be is what he actually is or even what he should be, were everything right with the world. If, however, what man possesses in the way of characteristics is enough, then one must conclude that "the proper study of mankind is man" because the only area of study that is either useful or realistically available to man is himself. Pope singles out scientific investigation as an area where mistaken ideas are pursued, and he sets up the same self-imposed discipline. The scientists should stay within the limits of the useful.

> Trace Science then, with Modesty thy guide;
> First strip off all her equipage of Pride,
> Deduct what is but Vanity, or Dress,
> Or Learning's Luxury, or Idleness;
> Or tricks to shew the stretch of human brain,
> Mere curious pleasure, or ingenious pain:
> Expunge the whole, or lop th' excrescent parts
> Of all, our Vices have created Arts:
> Then see how little the remaining sum,
> Which serv'd the past, and must the times to come!
>
> (II, 43–52)

There was wide agreement, in reaction to the supposedly extravagant expectations of scientists from Bacon on, that self-imposed limits were urgently necessary in scientific investigation.[14]

14. In addition to the notes in Mack, p. 61, see the following: "To soare after Inscrutable Secrets; to unlocke and breake open the closet of Nature, and to measure by our shallow apprehensions the deep and impenetrable Counsels of Heaven, which we should with a holy, fearful, and astonished Ignorance onely adore, is too bold and arrogant sacriledge, and hath much of that Pride in it, by which the Angels fell" (Edward Reynolds, *A Treatise of the Passions and Faculties of the Soul* [London, 1640], p. 499). "And yet is there any thing more Absurd and Impertinent in this, than in the present Supposition, to have a Man, who has so great a Concern upon his Hands as the Preparing for Eternity, all busie and taken up with *Quandrants*, and *Telescopes, Furnaces, Syphons*, and *Air-Pumps?*" (Norris, *Reflections*, pp. 142–43). "Learning does but serve to fill us full of Artificial Errors" (Sir Thomas Pope Blount, *Essays on Several Subjects* [London, 1697], p. 50).

John Norris, the enthusiastic English supporter of Malebranche, warns that man should not waste his time on speculation. His view is based on the idea that man does not have time to waste on such matters, that he should apply his time to saving his soul.

And so Learning and Knowledge are excellent things, and such as would deserve my Study, and my Time, had I any to *spare*, and were more at leisure; but not certainly when I have so great an Interest as that of my Final State depending upon the good use of it. My Business *now* is not to be *Learned*, but to be *Good*.[15]

Malebranche's own emphasis is on the illusory quality of what man can learn through extended intellectual inquiry, though his basic point is that science should be traced modestly.

But these *Great Genius's,* who pierce into the most *Mysterious Secrets* of Nature, who lift themselves in *Opinion* as high as *Heaven,* and descend to the bottom of the *Abyss,* ought to remember *what* they *are.* These great Objects, it may be, do but dazle them. The Mind must needs *depart* out of it self, to compass so many things; and this it can't do without *scattering* its Force.

Men came not into the World to be *Astronomers,* or *Chymists,* to spend their whole Life at the end of a *Telescope.* . . . What are they the wiser or happier for all this? . . .

Astronomy Chymistry, and most of the other Sciences, may be look'd on as proper Divertisements for a Gentleman. But Men should never be enamour'd with their *Gayety,* nor prefer them before the *Science* of *Humane Nature.* . . . The Mind must *pronounce* of all things, according to its *Internal Light,* without harkening to the false and confus'd *Verdict* of its *Senses* and *Imagination;* and whilst it examines all Humane Sciences by the *Pure Light* of Truth, which enlightens it, we doubt not to affirm it will disesteem most of them, and set a greater Price on that which teaches us *to know our selves,* than on all the other put together.[16]

This quotation from Malebranche includes most of Pope's restrictions on the desirability of keeping scientific investigation

15. Norris, *Reflections*, p. 141.
16. Malebranche, *Search after Truth*, 1:sig. A3r.

within bounds, and his hint that these men "ought to remember *what* they *are*" begins to suggest Pope's emphasis. That is, Pope aims at pride rather than the falsity of what might be discovered or the necessity to use the available time for more important purposes. Both conclude, however, that the proper study of mankind is man.

Pope's main thought is that men strive beyond themselves. In striving beyond themselves, they assume that they are greater and more important than they are ("Men would be angels, angels would be Gods"), and it is on this false assumption of their own importance that they base their indictment of God: he has not given them capacities suitable to their misconception of themselves. When they argue with providence in this manner, men cause themselves bitterness and frustration; therefore, Pope warns man to submit to his natural limitations.

The most singular and individualized attitudes toward reason to be found in the *Essay on Man* are not directed toward the thinking and reasoning processes. Little if anything is said about how to reason, except for occasional assertions about logical propriety. Common sense and common forms apparently rule the process. *Reason,* as Pope usually uses the word, is virtually personified. When the word is thus used, it means something like the capacity to reason, or perhaps even consciousness of one's own existence and mental processes. (Twentieth-century students will notice that two hundred years have done little if anything for the precision of the word, since the latest dictionaries give a multiplicity of definitions quite similar to Pope's own.) In Pope's system, just as self-love is a unified motivation of which each individual passion is a single mode of expression, so reason is a vague sort of consciousness; and each act of reasoning is one of its modes. Apparently some of what reason accomplishes is not, strictly speaking, conscious, for Pope says that reason performs for man the functions that instinct performs for beasts, and is "all these powers in one." It could be, of course, that Pope was ready to defend the position that all human activity is guided by specifically conscious observation, and when he counsels man to learn from the beasts, he gives examples of instinctual action in the beasts which man should observe and profit from (III, 170–83).

We probably cannot limit Pope's use of the word *reason* as unequivocally as we might like to, but we should be aware that he does mean by the term both a large function that includes most of consciousness and the processes of speculation by which problems are worked out. What is important to Pope's system is that reason (thought of in either of these ways) is not the predominant characteristic of man; it is not, as to many of his contemporaries it would have been, the man. "Two principles in human nature reign,/ Self-love to urge, reason to restrain." Although two principles reign in man, they do not reign equally, and Pope refers to reason as a "weak queen." When he switches metaphors, reason is "the card" by which the ship of man is guided as it is propelled by the winds of passion. The card, however, is a compass, a tool that man uses in order to distinguish and attain goals, goals urged primarily by self-love. It is with the comprehensive, personified functioning of reason rather than with the methods of ratiocination that Pope is primarily concerned.

The most important restrictions that he places on reason are: (1) that it is weak—specifically, weaker than self-love and the passions; (2) that it is essentially passive. It is a comparing power. The whole idea that what reason does is to compare is based on the assumption that reason receives sense impressions which represent reality to it (though reason's reality need not be ultimate or metaphysical reality, but only what helps the self to know or to cope with the world in which it lives). Reason's responsibility is to take the conscious perceptions which it receives and inform the self of their qualities. In order to do this it can only use material of which it becomes aware from outside, rather than originate its own reality. In other words, reason, when thought of in these terms, is a faculty for manipulating material; yet even within this conception, there is still room for controversy concerning the source of the impressions reason receives.

Pope's contemporaries were apparently agreed that one of the main functions of reason was to compare the objects of perception. There was less agreement, however, on what reason used for making its comparisons. Two quite different views were represented by the works by Malebranche and Locke already cited. Malebranche says that we compare "particular goods with the idea we have of Sovereign Goods, or with other particular goods," but to Locke the comparison of the more abstract "idea of Sovereign Goods" is omitted in favor of the comparison of one idea to another. The real difference here is that to Locke the material used in reasoning originates exclusively in sense experience, and to Malebranche the foundation of true knowledge is "seeing things in God," or a direct experience of truth through God, to which sense experience is a detriment. Peter Browne, in this particular, is a Lockean.[17]

> ... It appears the Ideas of Sensation are the only subject matter
> which the Mind hath to work upon, provided by God and Nature
> for the exercise of all its Powers and Faculties; and since they are
> the foundation and rough materials of all our most *Abstracted*
> Knowledge; out of which each Man raises a superstructure according
> to the different Turn of those Organs which are more immediately
> subservient to the Operations of the pure Intellect ... it will be
> convenient to say something concerning the several *Properties* of
> those Ideas.[18]

He then emphasizes his conviction that the reasoning process has no other materials with which to build, and also gives the view that reason is a manipulator rather than an originator.

---

17. Browne (whose book is directed most emphatically against John Toland's *Christianity Not Mysterious*) does not finally limit knowledge to ideas. To ideas, as has been noticed, he adds analogy. He defines ideas as the product of sense experience to be distinguished from notions and experiences resulting from the working of the mind on ideas.

18. Browne, pp. 87–88.

. . . The Soul, before there is some *Impression* of outward Objects upon the Senses, is a *Still* unactive Principle, unable to exert itself in any degree; it cannot form one Thought nor have the least consciousness even of its own Being.[19]

On the other hand, Malebranche agrees generally that reason is passive, but he lays stress upon the necessity to resist the information which is given to man by the senses.

Truths are found out, and all Sciences learn'd merely by the *Attention* of the Mind . . . 'tis our Duty constantly to withstand the Opposition the *Body* makes against the *Mind;* and to accustom our selves by degrees to *disbelieve* the *Reports* our Senses make concerning all circumambient Bodies, which they always represent, as worthy of our Application and Esteem, because we must never make *Sensible things* the Object of our Thoughts, or the Subject of our Employment.[20]

Malebranche's position is the result of a split between mind and body, and he regards the split as basic to any consideration of man. The senses are for the purpose of serving the body in its motive of self-preservation, but they are not for discovering truth.

For we have several ways demonstrated, that our *Senses, Imagination,* and *Passions,* are absolutely useless to the Discovery of *Truth* and *Happiness;* that on the contrary, they dazzle and seduce us on all occasions; and in general, that all the *Notices* the Mind receives through the *Body,* or by Means of some *Motions* excited in the *Body,* are all *false* and *confus'd,* with reference to the *Objects* represented by them; though they are extremely *useful* to the *Preservation* of the *Body,* and the *Goods* that are related to it.[21]

Truth, on the other hand, is to be found in "pure ideas of the mind."

But when a Man judges of things but by the pure *Ideas* of the *Mind,* carefully avoids the confus'd *Noise* of the Creatures, and retiring into himself, hears his *Sovereign Teacher* in the calm Silence of the Senses and Passions, he cannot possibly fall into Errour.[22]

19. Ibid., p. 88.
20. Malebranche, *Search after Truth,* 1:sig. A2v.
21. Ibid.
22. Ibid., 1:sig. A2r.

Peter Browne stands with Locke in denying any such capacity of the human mind or spirit to operate independent of the senses. Though his book was published in 1728, he at least considered the Malebranchian hypothesis to have some currency.

Thinking is by a general Mistake attributed to the *Pure* Spirit, exclusively of those material Organs without which it cannot exert one *Thought;* and in a necessary Conjunction with which, it performs all its Operations.[23]

Browne and Malebranche agree on the passivity of reason, and they agree that one of reason's most important functions is to compare, but they give two distinct possibilities regarding what reason is passive toward as it experiences things and how reason is made aware of those bits of experience it can regard as truth or reality. Pope is apparently quite near Browne's choice.

It is not, however, with the conflict between reason and the senses that Pope's most important conclusions regarding reason are concerned. The more important issue has to do with reason's relationship to the passions, and Pope concludes that reason, in the process of serving the whole creature, is subservient to self-love. Here he is reacting to a massive tradition that regarded man as primarily reasonable and asserted as self-evident the proposition that reason must ever predominate in a creature so constructed. Pope turns the idea around and asserts self-love to be predominant and reason to be the tool which self-love uses in order to attain its ends. The strength of reason is a separable issue, and most of what is important in the age's disputes over reason's capacity to guide men properly can be found in various controversies over the sufficiency of natural religion for man's needs.

The pervading issue in that controversy was the relationship between faith and reason in the acceptance of religious doctrines. That, at any rate, was the primary concern during most of the seventeenth century. Pope was not (in the *Essay on Man*)

23. Browne, p. 147.

concerned with the acceptance of religious doctrines, however; and while the controversy between the Anglican rationalists and their Catholic or Puritan adversaries will contribute characteristic ideas describing the limits of reason, an even more important group of works is to be found in the later discussion of this problem carried on between Anglican rationalists and that group of writers which the age often vaguely called deists.

When the Anglican rationalists were arguing with the Catholics and Puritans, all three groups agreed that the proper belief for humanity was something called Christianity, but all did not agree on the details of that belief or the bases upon which it was established. When the Anglican rationalists argued with the atheists they had only to convince them of the existence of God and the reasonableness of the Christian revelation. The deists accepted the existence of God and the desirability of a religion, but they questioned institutional Christianity's claim to be the necessary religion. They held natural religion (and therefore reason) to be a sufficient guide to action on earth. Here we can see the groundwork for a significant split in the direction of argument. Much of the time, in the controversy over natural religion, the issue is how men are to be motivated to lead virtuous lives. Is revelation necessary on this earth to make men moral, or can a moral mode of life be arrived at by the use of reason alone? There is, of course, another important question available, but it really plays no role in a system of natural religion that stays within its prescribed limitations. How are men to arrive at salvation?

Pope is satisfied with neither the skeptic's side nor the rationalist's pride; instead of isolating reason, he combines it with another principle called self-love. The division is not between soul and body, for reason and self-love are both parts of the mind. They are not conflicting or antagonistic elements since they are right for such a creature as man in the proportions Pope describes:

> Two Principles in human nature reign;
> Self-love, to urge, and Reason, to restrain;

> Nor this a good, nor that a bad we call,
> Each works its end, to move or govern all:
> And to their proper operation still,
> Ascribe all Good; to their improper, Ill.
>
> (II, 53–58)

In each case Pope elected to use an ambiguous term for his reigning principle. The ambiguity of *reason* as it refers to some general capacity as well as to the processes of reasoning has been noted. *Self-love* was, to Pope's contemporaries, even more ambiguous. Although the term could sometimes be taken to mean *selfishness*, it often meant little more than *self-preservation*, and when this was its meaning, the drive was agreed to be necessary to man's nature. Most important, by the second decade of the eighteenth century an earlier negative reaction to the concept of self-love had been overcome, and there was wide agreement that self-love was good or bad depending on its strength and the degree to which it was "enlightened." Pope takes the word thus disarmed and rearms it by asserting it to be stronger than reason in man's constitution, but he disarms it yet again by making strong self-love and weaker reason the proper combination for man as he is, in the world he inhabits.

The immediate concern of the present discussion is the way in which reason operates in its combination with predominant self-love.

> Self-love, the spring of motion, acts the soul;
> Reason's comparing balance rules the whole.
> Man, but for that, no action could attend,
> And, but for this, were active to no end;
> Fix'd like a plant on his peculiar spot,
> To draw nutrition, propagate, and rot;
> Or, meteor-like, flame lawless thro' the void,
> Destroying others, by himself destroy'd.
> Most strength the moving principle requires;
> Active its task, it prompts, impels, inspires.
> Sedate and quiet the comparing lies,
> Form'd but to check, delib'rate, and advise.

> Self-love still stronger, as its objects nigh;
> Reason's at distance, and in prospect lie:
> That sees immediate good by present sense;
> Reason, the future and the consequence.
> Thicker than arguments, temptations throng,
> At best more watchful this, but that more strong.
> The action of the stronger to suspend
> Reason still use, to Reason still attend:
> Attention, habit and experience gains,
> Each strengthens Reason, and Self-love restrains.
>
> (II, 59–80)

Reason's most essential responsibility is to restrain, that is, to curb the impetuosity of self-love so that those objects and actions may be avoided which seem good at first glance but are not finally desirable. In other words, it compares one thing with others. Reason in this way keeps self-love on a track that will produce a desired final or total effect, whereas self-love, if left alone, would go off in all directions and never accomplish anything. In the lines "Reason's comparing balance rules the whole" and "Sedate and quiet the comparing lies," Pope gives the double attitude in which one must see reason's activity of comparing. Reason, as it compares, is finally what regulates the movement of the whole creature; but it does its work in a passive rather than an active way.

One of Pope's most important images in this regard has been mentioned. Reason regulates man as a map or a compass that the self makes use of, rather than as a pilot who regulates a ship and himself determines its direction. Nautical tools do not determine the destination of the vessel but only the direction in which the ship must sail in order to attain the destination. In addition to comparing, reason checks, deliberates, and advises. All of these activities stress the certain quality Pope gives to reason, the quality of dealing with the material of its experience rather than inventing or originating ideas.

The general observation that reason is weak, and specifically that it is weaker than self-love, leaves the reader with the necessity of finding Pope's solution to a paradox. His solution is to adjust the system so that reason, with the qualities and limitations he describes, will be sufficient. For Pope the sufficiency is accomplished by giving reason aid from within the system or, one might better say, by cautioning reason to act within its proper sphere. Reason does not produce reality; it uses it. It acts on and manipulates the evidence of its surroundings.

In order to put reason in its proper perspective, Pope compares it with instinct. Instinct provides beasts with the proper motivations to fulfill their needs, and reason does the same service for man.

> How Instinct varies in the grov'ling swine,
> Compar'd, half-reas'ning elephant, with thine:
> 'Twixt that, and Reason, what a nice barrier;
> For ever sep'rate, yet for ever near!
> Remembrance and Reflection how ally'd;
> What thin partitions Sense from Thought divide. . . .
>   (I, 221–26)

Pope has in these lines suggested that memory is an essential characteristic of reason, and when memory is coupled with the comparing power, the two together constitute reason's distinctive mode of operation. Reason is able to compare the contents of the memory, and this gives it an advantage over the instinct of brute creation. The advantage is a relative one, for finally Pope asserts that reason and instinct are equal, that is, equal in the sense that each set of capacities does what it is intended to do for the needs of the creature ("Is not thy Reason all these pow'rs in one?" [I, 232]). Pope's most complete comparison of man's conscious capacities with those of beasts puts the emphasis on the advantages of instinct; but if one remembers that his purpose here, as elsewhere, is to humble pride, this emphasis is justified. Pope is reacting to the assurance voiced by prideful man that the universe and all the creatures in it are for man's benefit. The most important conclusion, however, is that reason and instinct are equally satisfactory to the creatures which possess them.

Whether with Reason, or with Instinct blest,
Know, all enjoy that pow'r which suits them best;
To bliss alike by that direction tend,
And find the means proportion'd to their end.
Say, where full instinct is th'unerring guide,
What Pope or Council can they need beside?
Reason, however able, cool at best,
Cares not for service, or but serves when prest,
Stays 'till we call, and then not often near;
But honest Instinct comes a volunteer;
Sure never to o'er-shoot, but just to hit,
While still too wide or short is human Wit;
Sure by quick Nature happiness to gain,
Which heavier Reason labours at in vain.
This too serves always, Reason never long;
One must go right, the other may go wrong.
See then the acting and comparing pow'rs
One in their nature, which are two in ours,
And Reason raise o'er Instinct as you can,
In this 'tis God directs, in that 'tis Man.

(II, 79–98)

The ambiguity of the case Pope presents in these lines also stands in some need of resolution. The directness and constancy with which instinct operates are in sufficient contrast with the laboriousness and fallibility of reason to make Pope's assurance that reason is right for the species possessing it rather paradoxical. The first question that would be likely to arise is, would not reason be a liability since it leaves man open to error, as instinct would not do? That question Pope does not answer because (presumably) the a priori argument from a necessarily full creation makes the question redundant. There is a relevant question remaining, however, and that is, how does a posteriori observation support our confidence in the a priori assertion that reason is what it should be? The question can only be answered by placing reason in its own context of operation. Of major importance would be a demonstration of the way or ways in which reason is supported by its surroundings so that it is aided in its tasks by material derived from the observation of its environment. That is to say, reason is not isolated and exposed to a hostile atmosphere, which would indeed make it of questionable value to man, but instead it has only to use the information provided it by nature (that is, to follow nature) in order to arrive at its proper end. Of the guides offered to reason by nature, perhaps the most basic is the experience of pleasure and pain.

Guides to Reason: Pleasure and Pain

The whole creature (or reason and self-love specifically) is motivated by the desire to achieve pleasure and avoid pain. Reason, therefore, is not required to decide whether to follow pleasure or pain. Its task is, rather, to determine what actions or objects will provide pleasure and which will, in the event, be painful; for self-love reacts to appearances and has no ability to predict the distant outcome of an action. There is no area in which reason would be led to resist pleasure or adopt a painful course. There is only the true determination of which actions will produce which results.

> Pleasure, or wrong or rightly understood,
> Our greatest evil, or our greatest good.
> (II, 91–92)

It is, again, not the simple assertion that men are motivated by pleasure and pain that could put Pope's system into one school of thought or another. One needs to know what variety of reactions Pope's contemporaries had to the theory that men are motivated in this way. In effect there is little difference between the assertion that men are motivated by pleasure and pain rather than abstract principles and the assertion that they are motivated entirely by self-love. (Contemporaries, indeed, frequently regarded the two assertions as equal.) Nevertheless, there is a clear spectrum of conclusions to be drawn from the assertion that men are motivated exclusively by pleasure and pain rather than abstract truth or categorical morality. At one extreme one might cite Benjamin Franklin's *Dissertation on Liberty and Necessity, Pleasure and Pain,* published in London in 1724. Franklin concludes that because men are motivated entirely by principles of pleasure and pain there is no such thing as virtuous action.

For since *Freedom from Uneasiness* is the End of all our Actions, how is it possible for us to do any Thing disinterested?—How can any Action be meritorious of Praise or Dispraise, Reward or Punishment, when the natural Principle of *Self-Love* is the only and the irresistible Motive to it?[24]

John Clarke of Hull uses the conviction that men are motivated entirely by pleasure and pain, which is to say self-love, to assert that morality is founded upon the rewards and punishments of a future state, since being truly moral inevitably involves painful and self-abnegating choices in this world. Without the expectation of a future state, human beings, motivated by pleasure and pain, could not possibly be induced to act contrary to present advantage.[25]

More commonly, the acknowledgement of the decisive sway of pleasure and pain was used to advance less extreme positions; however, these two somewhat radical assertions by Franklin and Clarke serve most clearly to demonstrate the nature of Pope's adaptation. Pope is closer to Clarke's position than he is to Franklin's, but the differences between Pope and Clarke are significant. Probably the only point which need be considered at length is Clarke's use of the urgent motivation toward pleasure and away from pain to support the necessity of a system of rewards and punishments to secure morality. Pope uses the idea in a benevolent system in which Clarke's need for something to mediate between self-love and social love when the two are in conflict does not apply because they never ultimately conflict. Clarke supports his argument by the necessity

24. Benjamin Franklin, *A Dissertation on Liberty and Necessity, Pleasure and Pain* (New York, 1930), p. 17.
25. See below, chapter 7, p. 178.

to protect from above the good of the whole creation, but Pope envisages a whole in which a system of compensations is at work that relieves God of the necessity to intervene in order to protect his creation.

The whole creation, as Pope describes it, is one in which self-love cannot be destructive, at least to the whole. Here one should remember that such motivations as self-love and pleasure and pain might be taken as supportive to a system rather than basic to it. Anthony Ashley Cooper, third Earl of Shaftesbury, is an important example of an author who presents another kind of system. He admits that rewards and punishments or the satisfaction of self-love may indeed by their additional support help a man to keep in the paths of virtue, but if such considerations are one's sole motivation, or the primary one, then there is no virtue in the case. To Pope, pleasure and pain are primary because there is in the system no conflict between them and virtue if the whole scheme can be seen. Shaftesbury, too, agrees that self-love and social love are in fact the same, but to him the fact is supportive to his insistence that the motivation to an action must come from social love if the action is to be called virtuous. At this point Pope and Shaftesbury part company, for Pope is explicit that "vice or virtue, self directs it still." On this subject Pope and John Clarke of Hull differ only at the point of Clarke's assurance that the next world is necessary to right the wrongs of this one, for the explicit purpose of much of Pope's point of view is to deny that very notion and to assert that this world needs no vindication through the medium of another.

To some extent the conclusion reached in a system acknowledging the dominant sway of pleasure and pain in human motivation depends on the definition of virtue. The assumption in the passage from Franklin quoted above is that nothing motivated by self-love can be called virtue (an assumption Franklin shares with Shaftesbury and Mandeville), and, since everything is motivated by self-love, virtue does not exist (a conclusion he shares with Mandeville). John Clarke agrees that everything is motivated by self-love, but he denies that the motivation destroys virtue. Virtue is doing what God commands, whether it is done to avoid a threat or not. Pope, taking the notion even further, leaves out the compliance with the will of God as a separate consideration. In Pope's system the creature will certainly obey the will of God (that is, the general will of God), but the creature may not know that it is doing so. Self-love, to Pope, is the will of God, but the motivation is not followed because the creature is conscious that God's will moves him; the motivation is followed for its own sake. Action thus motivated is not necessarily opposed to virtue, for nothing that is the will of God is of itself opposed to virtue. A misuse of a condition created by God might be vicious. Man, then, by his misuses, is the cause of vice, but God, by his superbly balanced system, is the cause of virtue.

Guides to Reason: Conscience

Even with the assurance that reason may turn the bias of man's inclinations "to good from ill," and with the suggestion that pleasure and pain (if rightly understood) will be a guide to good, Pope is sensible of the difficulty of telling good from evil in a world where they are closely intertwined. After working himself into the paradoxical conclusion that vice and virtue are so closely interwoven they can hardly be distinguished (II, 175–202), and adding the warning that reason is capable of rationalization in favor of the more immediately attractive of two forces, Pope finally has to ask and answer the difficult question:

> This light and darkness in our chaos join'd,
> What shall divide? The God within the mind.
> (II, 203–4)

A few lines later he refers the same responsibility of telling the difference between black and white to "your own heart," and he is apparently referring to the same faculty in both cases. The reader needs to know what human attribute Pope intends by the words "the God within the mind" and "your own heart."

The "God within the mind" has been identified as reason (see Mack, p. xxxviii), but it would probably be safer to give the phrase a less rational signification; Pope has certainly suggested that reason cannot be depended upon to divide the light and darkness. He has done this by stressing reason's weakness and by presenting the enigma in the first place, since it is surely reason that sees and is confused by the nearness of the two.

There is always a danger in giving this sort of metaphor a one-word solution, but Pope has given a fair clue to the meaning of "the God within the mind" by later using the words "ask your own heart." In the latter case he appears to be thinking about some form of conscience and, if this is the case, one can assume that "the God within the mind" is the same thing. In support of this interpretation, "the God within the mind" is so identified in the notes to the 1743 edition of the poem. It is possible that the note represents William Warburton's rather than Pope's interpretation and is therefore unreliable, but they did work on the edition together, and it seems unlikely that Pope would have passed on an incorrect interpretation when he had only to delete it. The poem itself, however, is the final authority, and the reliance on conscience, or something like it is more consistent with Pope's evaluation of reason as a "weak queen."

Pope is reflecting much of the thinking of his time when he assumes that there is some kind of natural capacity for telling good from bad.[26] In order to determine the spectrum of thought on the subject of conscience, one may recall John Locke's objection to innate conscience that has already been cited. Locke was seconded by, among others, William Wollaston, gentleman-philosopher and author of the popular *Religion of Nature Delineated*.

26. For some of the range of writers who cited a natural ability to tell good from bad, see the following: Malebranche, *Search after Truth*, 1:137; Anthony Ashley Cooper, 3d Earl of Shaftesbury, *Characteristics of Men, Manners, Opinions, Times,* ed. John M. Robertson, 2 vols. (London, 1900), 2:44; Butler, p. 45. For opposition to the idea in harmony with Locke, see Browne, pp. 227–28.

They, who contenting themselves with superficial and transient views, deduce the difference between good and evil from the *common sense* of mankind, and certain *principles* that are born with us, put the matter upon a very *infirm* foot. For it is much to be suspected there are no such *innate* maxims as they pretend, but that the impressions of education are mistaken for them. . . .[27]

Malebranche gives credit to the natural presence of such a guidance in "our own breast," but he also admits its lack of effect because of a corrupted nature. The actual presence of some such inner guidance is attested by "the father of English deism," Edward Herbert, Baron Herbert ("Herbert of Cherbury").

But the mark by which we distinguish good from evil is wholly the gift of nature; for it is not from the external world that we learn what we ought to follow, what we ought to avoid. Such knowledge is within ourselves; and this, in spite of what the authors say, is our own, and free, so that it cannot be subject to any limitation. Let us not continue to talk of a clean sheet, following the ancient school; for we can refer to the testimony of the inner feelings in due conformity, and it is therefore unnecessary to pay attention to these futile controversies.[28]

Pope never makes perfectly clear what he conceives this inner voice to be or how he conceives it to work, but the range of orthodoxy encompassed by the idea is wide (see note 26 above), from Herbert and Shaftesbury at the one end to Malebranche and Butler at the other. In Pope's poem there is, however, a crucial distinction: the difference between knowing what is good and being urged to do it. Pope's motivation toward good by principles of self-love (in adaptation of the tradition of Mandeville, Hobbes, and La Rochefoucauld) and the system where such motivation serves the best principles are things quite different from any of the systems ranging from Herbert and Shaftesbury to Butler. Man's ability to recognize good and evil intuitively, or in any other way, is irrelevant unless there is

27. Wollaston, pp. 35–36.
28. Herbert, p. 193.

some guarantee that he will do what he perceives to be good. (See below, pp. 119–25.)

Guides to Reason: Nature

The additional guide available to reason is nature. It can be considered as a separate guide and, of course, is also a broader term including the other guides within the system. Pope's use of the term *nature* has long been recognized as ambiguous; however, it seems realistic to notice that much of the time he uses the word as a rather simple personification of an abstraction. The abstraction is in many cases all of the characteristics and faculties born in the creature, including individual drives and differences as well as those common to the species. For example, the reader is told that each individual has a different set of senses, some stronger than others, and his interest or compulsion is directed by the one strongest sense.

> Hence diff'rent Passions more or less inflame,
> As strong or weak, the organs of the frame. . . .
> (II, 129–30)

A man receives these senses which dictate his ruling passion at birth, and the reader is told that "Nature [is] its mother." Seldom, if ever, does Pope mean by *nature* the physical material of the world. Nature is active and purposive. It appears to be an impulse within matter that is responsible for growth and direction, perhaps somewhat akin to the so-called vegetative soul commonly acknowledged by his contemporaries.[29]

29. See the following quotations:
> Nature to these, without profusion kind,
> The proper organs, proper pow'rs *assign'd* . . .
> (I, 179–80)
> Thus Nature *gives* us (let it check our pride)
> The virtue nearest to our vice ally'd . . .
> (II, 195–96)
> See plastic Nature *working* to this end . . .
> (III, 9)
> Thus God and Nature *link'd* the gen'ral frame,
> And *bade* Self-love and Social be the same.
> (III, 317–18)

Here, as elsewhere, emphasis should be placed on Pope's assertion that reason's primary function is to restrain the creature so that it will not destroy itself unawares. Therefore, the aids to reason in Pope's system are primarily boundaries or limitations to guide the restraining processes. Certainly Pope's use of nature as a guide to reason ("Suffice that Reason keep to Nature's road," and "Nature's road must ever be preferred")

> Know, all the good that individuals find,
> Or God and Nature *meant* to mere Mankind . . .
> > (IV, 77–78)
>
> There *deviates* Nature, and here wanders Will.
> > (IV, 112)
>
> Or Change admits, or Nature *lets* it fall . . .
> > (IV, 115)
>
> He sees, why Nature *plants* in Man alone
> Hope of known bliss, and Faith in bliss unknown . . .
> > (IV, 345–46)

I have italicized the verbs to show how Pope associates nature with intention and action. The introduction to the *Essay on Criticism* in the Twickenham edition is illuminating here, for I believe that much of what Pope says about nature in the two poems shows that the concept remained fairly stable in his mind (the quotation is referring to lines 68–73 of the *Essay on Criticism*): "The scarcely veiled analogy here is one between Nature and God: the attributions and formulae used are those traditionally reserved for the First Cause. Nature is one, eternal, immutable, and the source and end of all things. There is of course no suggestion of pantheism here. Instead, this is Pope's statement of the old idea that as God gives being to beings, so He makes causes to be causes, and thus grants to them the ability to participate in His power. That Nature which from one point of view may seem to have merely *received* the laws and order of its being, may from another be seen, by its participation in causality, as *conferring* these qualities. Pope is here concerned with a Nature which has a mysterious analogy to its Source in all its functioning" (Alexander Pope, *Pastoral Poetry and "An Essay on Criticism,"* eds. E. Audra and Aubrey Williams [London and New Haven, 1961], p. 221). This quotation emphasizes what I think needs emphasis, that Pope is dealing with an acknowledged mystery. He is not bungling or missing the implication of his own ideas. The significant further step that he takes in the *Essay on Man* is to be found in the lines "All are parts of one stupendous whole,/Whose body Nature is and God the soul." Here he shows (no less mysteriously) that he has come to think of nature as manifesting itself in this plastic (that is formative) manner, analogous to the way in which the body works independently of the soul yet is guided as a totality by it.

does not escape the equivocal use of the term common during the period, or, indeed, for centuries before.[30] It is also worthwhile to notice that he personifies a force rather than an object.

When Pope gives to reason the responsibility to restrain the creature, he means that reason must discover the creature's natural limits and demonstrate the urgency of operating within them.

> The bliss of Man (could Pride that blessing find)
> Is not to act or think beyond mankind. . . .
> (I, 189–90)

Pope's insistence that man must not try to be more—or less—than a man, the assurance that he must stay within his nature, requires that, within his system, some clear indication is available to man, and to his reason, of what his nature is; for the warning itself implies that man *can* think or act beyond mankind, even though he may not succeed in making himself happy by doing so. One evident way in which reason can determine the nature and limits of man is to observe what is pleasurable and painful to him.

> Suffice that Reason keep to Nature's road,
> Subject, compound them, follow her and God.
> Love, Hope, and Joy, fair pleasure's smiling train,
> Hate, Fear, and Grief, the family of pain;
> These mix'd with art, and to due bounds confin'd,
> Make and maintain the balance of the mind:
> The lights and shades, whose well accorded strife
> Gives all the strength and colour of our life.
> (II, 115–22)

Nature is responsible for all of man's most powerful and compelling motives, and for this reason alone it would be necessary to heed her advice. Nature gives each man his ruling passion,

---

30. The notion that the term was frequently a personification is supported by A. O. Lovejoy and George Boas, "Genesis of the Conception of 'Nature' as Norm," *Primitivism and Related Ideas in Antiquity* (Baltimore, 1935), p. 13; Wollaston, p. 155; Richard Boulton, *The Theological Works of the Honourable Robert Boyle, Esq., Epitomiz'd* (London, 1715), 2:91.

and nature gives "the virtue nearest to our vice ally'd" (II, 196). Nature gives the feeling of sympathy which moves man to help the creatures around him, and it also gives the individual differences which keep the whole creation functioning ("All Nature's diff'rence keeps all Nature's peace" (IV, 56). Finally nature gives man the hope and faith which make his position bearable, and, since nature gives nothing in vain, the hope will prove justified.

> He sees, why Nature plants in Man alone
> Hope of known bliss, and Faith in bliss unknown:
> (Nature, whose dictates to no other kind
> Are giv'n in vain, but what they seek they find)....
> (IV, 345–48)

The general idea that reason can examine nature to discover how man should act, or that truth can be discovered in nature, was capable of a considerable range of use.[31] The most important distinction has been discussed with Pope's reference to conscience as "the God within the mind." For purposes of interpretation, nature and "the God within the mind" need not be considered as separate counsels; though Pope does not specifically relate them, this inner light is certain to be a part of nature since it represents a natural attribute of the individual. Pope would again, then, be referring to the presence in man of certain attitudes which come, at least loosely, under the heading of innate capacities.[32] Nevertheless, there is some degree to which Pope is recommending nature not as human nature but as an operating and normative force outside of man.

Writers contemporary with Pope recommended nature as a source of guidance from at least two important bases. To one

31. See the following secondary sources: Basil Willey, *The Eighteenth Century Background* (London, 1940), p. 2; Lovejoy and Boas, p. 103; Margaret Mary Fitzgerald, *First Follow Nature: Primitivism in English Poetry* (New York, 1947), p. vii; Paul Hazard, *European Thought in the Eighteenth Century*, trans. J. Lewis (New Haven, 1945), p. 113.

32. Pope may be referring to some such voice in the following lines: "Nature that Tyrant checks; he only knows,/And helps, another creature's wants and woes" (III, 51–52).

group, nature put into man affections for what is good or benevolent. Both Shaftesbury and Butler rely in different ways and to different degrees on this natural capacity. At an extreme, this position would counsel man to do what is natural to him, although finding out what is natural might be no easy task after the damages of education and the corruptions of society. Pope, of course, refers even the natural sympathy with fellow creatures to man's "learned hunger" so that he never abandons the guidance of self-love to rely on a benevolence abstracted from personal gratification.

To other writers a recommendation of nature as a source of guidance was based on the assurance that real and eternal differences of things (the basis of all moral action) existed in nature. Reason need only consult the truths of the universe to discover what is to be done. What is to be done is what is true. This position undoubtedly involves some substantial ability to reason abstractly in order to arrive at the truths lying in nature's storehouse; but more than anything else, it depends on the conviction that the truth, if known, will attract man and motivate him.

Since Pope relies on a difference between good and bad as plain as black and white, and since man reacts with hate to the mien of vice upon first seeing, Wollaston's *Religion of Nature Delineated* will again provide a useful comparison. Wollaston says that man must act in accord with the truth that is to be found in the nature of things.

Therefore nothing can interfere with any proposition that is true, but it must likewise interfere with nature (the nature of the relation, and the natures of the things themselves too), and consequently be *unnatural*, or *wrong in nature*. So very much are those gentlemen mistaken, who by *following nature* mean only complying with their bodily inclinations, tho in opposition to truth, or at least without any regard to it. Truth is but a conformity to nature: and to follow nature cannot be to combat truth.[33]

33. Wollaston, p. 17.

Wollaston admits the difficulty of finding real truth, but essential to his system is the assurance that it can be done.

> It must be confest there is a *difficulty* as to the means, by which we are to consult our own preservation and happiness; to know what those are, and what they are with respect to us. . . . Our ignorance of the true natures of things, of their operations and effects in such an irregular distempered world . . . deprive us of certainty in these matters.[34]

He warns of the danger in following nature in a sense other than he uses it, but recommends it if it means "treating things as being what they in nature are, or according to truth."

> They who place all in *following nature,* if they mean by that phrase acting according to the natures of things (*that is,* treating things as being what they in nature are, or according to truth) say what is right. But this does not seem to be their meaning. And if it is only that a man must follow his own nature, since his nature is not purely rational, but there is a part of him, which he has in common with brutes, they appoint him a guide which I fear will mislead him, this being commonly more likely to prevail, than the rational part.[35]

Wollaston's split of the rational from the brute part of man shows the point at which he most strongly differs from Pope.

Finally, Wollaston's position (though it is submitted to a good deal of qualification) is that reason is superior to sense. "*In a word,* no man doth, or can pretend to believe his senses, when he has a reason against it: which is an irrefragable proof, that reason is above sense and controlls it."[36] It is, therefore, reason which must rule man's actions when he is properly guided. This means that, while Wollaston does recommend following nature in a sense, he does so because truth exists in the nature of things.

> It is plain, that reason is of a commanding nature: it injoins this, condemns that, only allows some other things, and will be paramount

34. Ibid., p. 23.
35. Ibid., pp. 34–35.
36. Ibid., p. 95.

... if it is at all. Now a being, who has such a determining and governing power so placed in his nature, as to be essential to him, is a being certainly framed to be governed by that power. It seems to be as much designed by nature, or rather the Author of nature, that rational animals should use their reason, and steer by it; as it is by the shipwright, that the pilot should direct the vessel by the use of the rudder he has fitted to it. The rudder would not be there, if it was not to be used: nor would reason be implanted in any nature only to be not cultivated and neglected. And it is certain, it cannot be used, but it must command: such is its nature.[37]

Wollaston's insistence that reason must act in accord with some kind of abstract truth, and that reason will be able to control the individual, is far beyond Pope's less sanguine expectations.

The Christian rationalist Nathanael Culverwell represents a variation on this general notion that is somewhat closer to Pope's position but still depends on a rational guidance too strong to be put into Pope's context. Culverwell carries on his discussion in terms of the law of nature (it performs, as the "candle of the lord" within men, most of the functions Pope or Wollaston expect from reason and nature in combination). Reason, in Culverwell's thought, apprises the soul of nature's law.

So that *Reason* is the Pen by which *Nature* writes this Law of her own composing; This Law 'tis publisht by Authority from heaven, and Reason is the Printer: This eye of the soul 'tis to spy out all dangers and all advantages, all conveniences and disconveniences in reference to such a being, and to warne the soul in the Name of its Creator, to fly from such irregularities as have an intrinsecal and implacable malice in them, and are prejudicial and destructive to its *Nature*, but to comply with, and embrace all such acts and objects as have a native comeliness and amiablenesse, and are for the heightning and ennobling of its being.[38]

Insofar as Culverwell concentrates on those acts which are

37. Ibid., p. 88.
38. Nathanael Culverwell, *An Elegant and Learned Discourse of the Light of Nature* (London, 1654), pp. 59–60.

destructive to the nature of the creature, he is close to Pope, but he is more likely to emphasize the idea that such a creature as man is bound by a law to which he can refer as an authority.

The Law of Nature is that Law which is intrinsecal and essential to a rational creature; and such a Law is as necessary as such a creature; for such a creature as a creature has a superiour, to whose Providence and disposing it must be subject; and then as an intellectual creature 'tis capable of a moral government, so that 'tis very suitable and connatural to it to be regulated by a Law; to be guided and com-manded by one that is infinitely more wise and intelligent then it self is; and that mindes its welfare more than it self can.[39]

Culverwell's theory is similar to Butler's in positing a quality in things which makes the soul respond to them in a positive or negative way. For Pope, men respond positively or nega-tively to actions or things because of the way these things affect self-love rather than from an affection for the abstract good-ness or badness in the things themselves. Culverwell, too, posits the notion that men naturally love some actions and hate others. He introduces the good of the individual as the source, but finally his emphasis is on the will of God in an essentially intellectual system of the universe (to borrow Cudworth's orotund phrasing).

There is some good so proportionable and nutrimental to the being of man, and some evil so venemous and destructive to his nature, as that the God of Nature does sufficiently antidote and fortifie him against the one and does maintain and sweeten his essence with the other. There is so much harmony in some actions, as that the soul must needs dance at them; and there is such an harsh discord and jarring in others, as that the soul cannot endure them. Therefore the learned Grotius does thus describe the Law of Nature. . . . The Law of Nature is a streaming out of Light from the Candle of the Lord, powerfully discovering such a deformity in some evil, as that an intellectual eye must needs abhor it; and such a commanding beauty in some good, as that a rational being must needs be enamoured with it; and so plainly showing that God stamp't

39. Ibid., p. 30.

and seal'd the one with his command, and branded the other with his disliking.[40]

Culverwell uses *the obvious qualities* of things as the basis upon which reason fills in the whole law of nature.

Now these first and radical principles are wound up in some such short bottoms as these. *Bonum est appetendum, malum est fugiendum; Beatitudo est quaerenda.* . . . And reason thus . . . by warming and brooding up these first and oval principles of her own laying, it being it self quicken'd with an heavenly vigour, does thus hatch the Law of Nature.[41]

Finally, then, the power of reason to do this dialectical job is essential.

This matter of the relationship between things and our attractions to them is of such importance to Pope's whole system as to warrant an extended examination of an urgent controversy that was taking place while Pope was working, at least on the final stages of the *Essay*. This controversy will show one way in which the issues were sorted. It would be difficult to overestimate the importance of the doctrinal conflict between the school of thought that held the reason of things to be the cause and basis of morality and that which insisted upon the will of God as the foundation stone.

"The reason of things" is a curious and rather awkward phraseology, but it is so frequently encountered in the period that it becomes virtually a single term. "The reason of things" refers to relationships between and among the creatures and objects of creation that supply the reasons why some acts are good, or moral, and others are bad, or immoral. The least equivocal example would be the fact that pain is the result of certain actions, and pain is undesirable by the very nature of the sensible creatures of the world. Those actions that cause pain, therefore, are clearly bad, or immoral, not because God has made a commandment to that effect (though such a com-

40. Ibid., pp. 36–37.
41. Ibid., p. 47.

mandment might be a supplementary or enforcing measure), but because of the essential character of the creatures and the consequences of their actions. The goodness or badness of an act is, then, based on the reason of things. The age itself seldom cut through the details to the central issue, and the arguments frequently give metaphysical reasons for the positions the authors defend even though the authors may be largely motivated by such political considerations as the authority of the established church.

Closely parallel to the theological or philosophical argument concerning the foundation of morality, runs the political issue turning on the same hinge; the issue is whether men owe allegiance to authority or to their own reasonable awareness of the realities of the world. Hobbes attempted to decide this question by assessing man and demonstrating that organizations that were the product of man would have characteristics in harmony with the creature that made them. Although no writer was likely in this period to confess a similarity to Hobbes, a focus of attention on the qualities of man, and an emphasis on the selfishness of the creature, was found to be helpful when one wanted to show that man needed some strong authority to keep him in submission. It is for this reason that no matter how the two sides may qualify their positions and begin to sound like the opposition, the whig-latitudinarian-deist position basically insists on man's reasonableness, and the tory-establishment position regards him as a creature of passion. For in the hands of the skilful arguers, the fulcrum of the argument is not what man knows but what dictates his action. On both sides there are qualifications and softenings, but to the writers who understand the argument, the one side insists on the triumph of reason and the other on the decisive sway of self-interest.

A particularly good embodiment of this conflict is the controversy between Daniel Waterland and Arthur Ashley Sykes around Samuel Clarke's posthumous *Exposition of the Church-Catechism* which had been seen through the press by his brother in 1729.[42] The controversy began in 1730 with Waterland's *Remarks Upon Dr. Clarke's Exposition of the Church-Catechism.* Waterland's pamphlet evidently attracted some attention since the British Museum Catalogue lists a third edition still dated 1730. Most of Waterland's discussion deals with a drift toward Socinianism in Dr. Clarke's comments; however, toward the end he objects to Clarke's assertion that the sacraments have value not in themselves as positive duties, but rather in their instrumental value as a means toward virtue. He argues, *"Moral Virtues* are rather to be consider'd as a *Means* to an End, because they are *previous* Qualifications for the Sacraments, and have no proper Efficacy towards procuring Salvation till they are improv'd and render'd acceptable

42. The controversy was quite extensive. See the following: Daniel Waterland, *Remarks upon Dr. Clarke's Exposition of the Church-Catechism* (London, 1730) (this went into a third edition the same year). Arthur Ashley Sykes, *An Answer to the Remarks upon Dr. Clarke's Exposition of the Church-Catechism* (London, 1730) (went into a second edition the same year). Daniel Waterland, *The Nature, Obligation, and Efficacy, of the Christian Sacraments, Considered* . . . (London, 1730) (went into a second edition the same year). Arthur Ashley Sykes, *A Defence of the Answer to the Remarks upon Dr. Clarke's Exposition of the Church-Catechism* (London, 1730). Daniel Waterland, *A Supplement to the Treatise, entituled, The Nature, Obligation, and Efficacy of the Christian Sacraments Considered* (London, 1730). Arthur Ashley Sykes, *The True Foundations of Natural and Reveal'd Religion Asserted* . . . (London, 1730).
   Others entered into the fray: Thomas Chubb, *The Comparative Excellence and Obligation of Moral and Positive Duties, Fully Stated and Considered* . . . (London, 1730). Thomas Chubb, *A Discourse Concerning Reason, With Regard to Religion and Divine Revelation. . . . To Which are added, Some Reflections upon the Comparative Excellency and Usefullness of Moral and Positive Duties, Occasioned by the Controversy that has Arisen* . . . *Upon the Publication of Dr. Clarke's Exposition* . . . (London, 1731). T. Emlyn, *A Letter to the Revd Dr. Waterland, Occasion'd by Remarks on Dr. Clarke's Exposition* . . . (London, 1730). N. Nichols, *An Impartial Review of the Controversy Concerning the Comparative Excellence &c. of Moral and Positive Duties* (London, 1731). Phillips Glover, *A Discourse Concerning Virtue and Religion, occasioned by some late writings* (London, 1731). Edward Underhill, *Celsus Triumphatus: Or, Moses Vindicated* . . . (London, 1732). A beautifully effective, forceful statement on Waterland's side of the question is Thomas Johnson, *An Essay on Moral Obligation* (London, 1731).

by these *Christian* Performances. By *Moral Virtues* only, we shall never ordinarily come at Christ, nor at Heaven, nor to the Presence of God. . . ."[43] Real religion, says Waterland, is a matter of submission rather than reasoning. Men should obey God's commands because they have been made rather than because men regard them as reasonable.

> The Truth of the Case, as I conceive, lies here: The *Love of God* is the *first* and *great* Commandment: And Obedience to his *positive* Institutions is an Exercise of that Love; and it is sometimes the *noblest* and *best* Exercise of it, shewing the greater Affection, and prompter Resignation to the divine Will. He is a proud and sawcy Servant that will never obey his Master but where he sees the *Reason* of the Command.[44]

The case that Waterland makes is quite modest. He distinguishes between moral duties (those that are obligatory because of the consequences they bring upon the creatures involved in the actions they recommend or discourage) and positive duties (actions that are obligatory because they were commanded by God to be done). He merely wants to assert that a general or total preference of moral duties to positive duties should not be stated and that sometimes positive duties may be of greater importance, more moral, or, perhaps, more holy. Positive duties are vital to Christianity because of the necessity of baptism and the eucharist to salvation. Of course, the distinction between the two types of duty has a close relationship to that between justification by faith and justification by works. One encounters one side positing a man who lives a life of wild sin and debauchery but who believes in the divinity of Christ and the other side giving the example of the hypocrite who does charitable works but has no love of God in his heart. These are the rhetorical flourishes which no one who defends either side will admit to be illustrative of the working of his position.

43. Waterland, *Remarks*, p. 85.
44. Ibid., pp. 86–87.

There is, however, an issue of genuine importance involved. The issue is whether the moral man does what he does because he sees good reasons for doing it or because he submits to a superior authority. Is the purpose of religion to inspire and enable men to lead moral lives, that is, treat one another well, or is there another element that involves genuine but symbolic submission to a higher authority for its own sake? If, Waterland insists, men think they merit salvation by their virtue, their pride will betray them.[45]

Arthur Ashley Sykes was a friend to Dr. Clarke's and an avid controversialist, and he entered the lists against Waterland with *An Answer to the Remarks upon Dr. Clarke's Exposition of the Church-Catechism,* which also went into a second edition in 1730. In his defense of the *Exposition* he was defending his own honor as well as that of the school of thought to which he belonged. Waterland's attack was, or could be interpreted to be, an attack on their Christianity. In his final summary Waterland had said, "It is plain enough that *Arianism* is but the Dupe to *Deism,* as Deism again is to *Atheism,* or Popery. . . ."[46] To some extent, then, the argument will again be sidetracked from what is correct to what is Christian.

With the supposed Arianism of Sykes' (or Clarke's) argument the present chapter is not concerned; the controversy quickly narrows down to a more crucial issue. To answer Waterland's claim that positive and moral duties should not be compared in favor of the moral, and even the modest assertion that positive duties may *sometimes* be of superior value, Sykes asserts, "As there are positive Institutions appointed by our Saviour, these are so far from being 'perfective of Virtue,' that they are nothing but certain *Means to that End.* . . ."[47] This he quickly follows by his key point: "That nothing *can* have a more proper and immediate Efficacy, to make us acceptable to God, than Moral Virtue. For what is it can make a reasonable Creature acceptable to God, but the imitation of

45. Ibid., p. 88.
46. Ibid., p. 94.
47. Sykes, *Answer to the Remarks,* p. 74.

God; the acting reasonably, and suitably to those Powers which we have?"[48] One can hardly suppose that he did not know Waterland's answer—preferable to imitation is obedience.[49]

Sykes narrows the issue down more clearly in his final paragraph.

To tell us, that "Natural Religion as it is called, will soon be what every Man pleases, and will shew itself in little else but *natural depravity*," were it not for the Scripture, is plainly saying, that Morality is not in itself capable of Evidence; that 'tis not founded upon the Reasons of Things, and that the Religion of Nature is not capable of being proved obligatory upon reasonable Creatures. The Man that can say this, seems not to know what Natural Religion, or its Obligations are founded on; and whilst he is ignorant of them, He may talk of Revelation as a Rule, but will scarce ever be able to apply it to the Explication of any Command or Prohibition contain'd therein.[50]

Waterland replied in *The Nature, Obligation, and Efficacy, of the Christian Sacraments, Considered....* This pamphlet also went into a second edition in 1730. Although most of the discussion is taken up with the relative importance of positive and moral obligations, the question of major importance is the binding source of any obligation—not the fact that a man is obliged, but the force that makes him submit to his obligation. Waterland's key assertion might have been taken directly from Hobbes: "Where *no Law is, there is no Transgression*."[51] He argues that those (Dr. Clarke and others) who fancy an "*obliging* and binding Force in the Nature and Reasons of Things, considered as previous, or antecedent to all Laws, natural or revealed" make a very weak case, for one must resolve "all Obligation into some divine Law, natural or revealed."[52] Here he refers the reader to John Clarke of Hull's

48. Ibid., p. 75.
49. Waterland, *Nature, Obligation*, p. 42.
50. Sykes, *Answer to the Remarks*, pp. 82–83.
51. Waterland, *Nature, Obligation*, p. 16.
52. Ibid.

The Foundation of Morality in Theory and Practice, so we see that he is attempting to narrow the discussion to what is really going to be the crux of the argument, that is, what determines men to action.

The motivation to action, he insists, is a thing quite separate from perception of qualities in objects that do not affect the perceiver directly. Here, however, he is at an earlier stage of the argument. He is saying that the evaluative distinction made by his adversaries between moral and positive duties is not valid because all duties are in fact positive since they all depend upon God's command. All that human beings need to know is that commands have been given. They do not need to know why.

> For the Will of God in these Cases is our immediate Rule to go by, and is the Ground and Measure of all Obligation. Unerring Wisdom has Reasons by which it constantly steers; and we cannot doubt but where God lays the greatest Stress, there are the greatest Reasons. But it will be enough for any Creature, in such Cases, to know that divine Wisdom insists upon it, and strictly requires it: For that alone is sufficient, without knowing more, to create the strictest and strongest Obligation.[53]

Here the issue should be clear. There is no point in using the reason of things as the basis of morality because the question that must be answered is, when man has seen the reason of things, what will compel him to do what is reasonable? Waterland bears down on Sykes' quotation given above to summarize the force of his whole argument.

> . . . however Morality might subsist in Theory (which I allowed before) it can never subsist in *Practice,* but upon a Scripture-foot. And the Reason which I before gave, and now repeat, is a very plain one, *viz.* that Scripture once removed, there will be no *certain* Sanctions to bind Morality upon the Conscience, no clear Account of Heaven or Hell, or a future Judgment to inforce it. . . .[54]

53. Ibid., pp. 17–18.
54. Ibid., pp. 82–83.

At this point Waterland's whole position is clear. Man is a creature who acts only from self-love (John Clarke's theory, of which Waterland approves); therefore, morality is made obligatory to man because he is commanded to act well and is threatened with punishment if he does not obey. His self-love, then, makes him choose heaven rather than hell and pursue what is necessary to secure his choice. The basis of morality is not reason, though morality may be reasonable.

With the issue thus narrowed, Sykes prepared *A Defence of the Answer to the Remarks upon Dr. Clarke's Exposition of the Church-Catechism.* His position is that morality is based on the relationship of things to one another, and since that relationship is immutable, so that even God cannot make things to be what they are not, there is no arbitrary will in the case.[55] The laws come from the reason of things rather than vice versa. If Waterland were correct in his placing morality in the will of God, moral good could have been made to consist of injustice and ingratitude. But since God must do what is best, we may see that God is *obliged* to do it; therefore, the basis of morality is that obligation rather than an act of will.

Sykes deals in little detail with the essence of Waterland's position, and his whole case is summed up in one sentence: "The religion of nature is capable of being shewn to be obligatory upon reasonable creatures."[56] It is not Sykes' intention to deny the value of Christianity, nor was that the intention of Samuel Clarke. They say that Christianity is useful to such a poor sinful creature as man, but to Waterland and many of his school this was tantamount to saying that Christianity is not *necessary* but only suplementary—an assertion, they believed, that led inevitably to deism. The willingness of men like Samuel Clarke

55. This does not mean that God could not have made things differently but that, given things as they are, the relationships among them are a product of existence. Sykes' school liked to use mathematics to illustrate the point. Not even God could make $2 + 2$ equal 5; $2 + 2$ equals 4 is a fact of existence. The argument is, of course, exactly the same as the one used to prove that God must form the best possible world.

56. Sykes, *Defence of the Answer*, p. 93.

and Sykes to divest Christianity of much of its mystery in order to make the positive gain of what seemed to them nearly mathematical certainty can be easily understood, but the reasons for Waterland's alarm must be equally evident.

Waterland answered Sykes yet again in *A Supplement to the Treatise, entituled, The Nature, Obligation, and Efficacy of the Christian Sacraments Considered.* This time he manages to get his charge down far less equivocally: Man will not be obliged by reasonableness, because he is motivated solely by self-love. He again refers the reader to the treatise of John Clarke of Hull. To some extent the argument about obligation is semantic, but that need not betray the reader into thinking that it lacks substance. In order to make God's freedom of will secure, those on Waterland's side of the argument (the argument is familiar from Leibniz) are not prepared to think of a necessary consequence as an obligation. One can only be obliged by a superior power who enforces the obligation. What one does because it is his nature to do it does not come under the same head. God cannot be obliged to observe the fitness of things but will do so anyway. Man, on the other hand, must be obliged because he operates not from reason but another principle.

All that these general *Fitnesses* mean, is, that they are good for Mankind, and that the Observance of them promotes the common Happiness: And yet it is very certain that every Man may, must, and cannot but pursue his own Happiness, and flee Misery as such. It is *fitting,* and *reasonable,* and *just,* that a Man should love and serve himself, *equally* at least with others: And it is *unfitting, unreasonable,* and *unjust* (were it practicable) for a Man to love his Neighbour *better* than himself. There is no *Wisdom,* or *Virtue,* in being wise for others only, and not for one's self also, first or last: Neither can any Man be obliged to it. Well then, let us imagine *Fitnesses* to be the Rule to go by, and no *Deity* at the Head of them, to bind and inforce them: It may be *fit* for a Man to observe them as far as is consistent, or co-incident with his Temporal Happiness: And that will be no *Virtue,* nor *Duty,* but Self-Interest only, and *Love* of the World. But if he proceeds farther to sacrifice his own temporal Happiness to the *Public*, that indeed will be *Virtue* and *Duty* on the Supposition that *God* requires it, but without it, it is Folly and Madness. There is neither *Prudence*, nor *good Sense*, and consequently no *Virtue*, in preferring the Happiness of others *absolutely* to our own; that is to say, without Prospect of a future *Equivalent*.[57]

Since God guarantees that we will not finally be losers by sacrificing our own immediate good to the good of the whole, sacrificing our present good is sound. Otherwise, nothing could induce man to accept such a principle. God can act according to the rules of abstract logic because he is not in danger of being hurt by it. Man is in quite a different position.

It is *fit* for God alone, it is his pecu[liar] Prerogative and Perfection, to adhere constantly to the Rules of *Truth* and *Goodness,* without *Obligation*, without *Law*. He is out of the Reach of Pain and Misery; and his Happiness can never interfere with the common Felicity. But *Creatures* may run Risques (all Creatures, more or less) and want both to be *bound* by Law, and to be *secured* by the same, as often as their temporal Happiness may interfere with the publick Interest. In such Cases, the Rules of Virtue would be no Rules to *Them*, because not *reasonable* in their Circumstances, till God by annexing Happiness and Misery to the Observance and Non-observance of them, turns the Scale, and makes them *eligible*, fit to be practis'd in all Circumstances whatever. Thus *Virtue* is rendered *obligatory* to all Creatures, and indeed is made *Virtue* to them . . . when it would be otherwise Folly and Distraction.[58]

Waterland makes it clear that the goodness or wisdom of the moral law is not in dispute, but the obligation to obey it is. Men do not obey because the law is good but because they submit to authority and its system of threat and reward, the real foundation of morality.

With the *Supplement,* Waterland's contribution to the controversy was at an end, but Sykes would not let the problems rest. *The True Foundations of Natural and Reveal'd Religion*

57. Waterland, *Supplement*, pp. 8–9.
58. Ibid., pp. 11–12.

Asserted is a restatement of his principles, but clearly the controversy is at a permanent standstill. The key, though not the acknowledged, assertion of the whole controversy is amenable to assertion but apparently not proof. That assertion, to repeat, is on the one side that man is a reasonable creature and on the other that he is not; but when the reader asks what is at stake in the argument, the answer is not "the actions of men." In fact, because there is substantial if not total agreement on the content of the moral laws, what the argument constitutes is a defense and attack (at least by logical extension) on the established church.

The argument itself is the proverbial pebble dropped into a pond. It is not yet known precisely what relationship this argument has to major distinctions between the Whig and Tory political philosophies and the justification of the Revolution of 1688 (as well as that of 1645). The present author is at work on the problem, and I have already suggested that I am quite certain there was some perceivable tendency for political theorists to form into groups similar to those represented by Waterland and Sykes, one grounding the need for authority on human depravity and the other urging human reason in defense of freedom from arbitrary rule or implicit faith. We have learned in the past twenty years or so not to make large generalizations about what either Whigs or Tories believed, and I do not mean to suggest that a man's position on whether human beings are predominantly passionate or reasonable could be taken as a valid criterion for party membership. I do believe, however, that further investigation will show that Tory rhetoric frequently found the views of Waterland more useful (transmuted into political rather than religious coinage), and that the Whig writers relied more heavily on Sykes' evaluation of man.

That this should be so can hardly be surprising; the directions are rather obvious. One sometimes falls into the eighteenth-century fear of the ideas of La Rochefoucauld, Hobbes, and Mandeville, the men who seemed the radicals and system-wreckers; but one should not be confused by their method or the curious obliqueness of their attack. It was they who provided the strongest as well as the liveliest material for defending the political and clerical status quo. It was they who believed that the world runs the way it does because men are what they are, so that a notion that man's world may change by force of will was, for them, inadequate. Sykes condemned Waterland's moral foundation as the "morality of a Highwayman, or Pickpocket, to be *just* only for fear of the Gallows."[59] If Waterland had been a less moderate arguer, he would have answered that men are highwaymen and pickpockets, and it is the gallows alone that keeps society safe; it is not the good laws that subdue men to law and order, but the punishments attached to them.

There is so much in Waterland's whole structure of thought that is at the very heart of Pope's assessment of man's reason that one must restrain his enthusiasm over similarities to notice the most telling and decisive difference. Since Pope is constructing a system of natural religion and therefore explicitly excluding all revelation, he does not have available to him the key conclusion of Waterland's whole system, the necessity of rewards and punishments to restrain a creature who is predominantly self-loving. Instead, Pope puts that restraint within the system by making self-love and social love the same, so that present fulfillment, not future rewards, is the motivation of predominant self-love. This middle road stems from Pope's willingness to sacrifice the traditional, rigorous definition of virtue and to give God the credit for all the beauty and harmony and benevolence to be found in the system.

59. Sykes, *True Foundation*, p. 26.

5

The Vindication of the Passions

Just as he committed himself to defend weak reason at the same time he declared it weak, so Pope committed himself to defend strong and governing passions when he admitted that the passions were dominant. Generally Pope's age took one of two courses when describing the functioning of the passions. Most writers, however they evaluated the strength of the passions, insisted that reason was stronger and could, therefore, rule if it would. Some others were less optimistic about the power of reason. They described man as a creature dominated by his passions and were skeptical of the notion that there was any force in man or nature capable of effectively governing or conquering them. Pope did not admit reason to be stronger than the passions in his description of man, but neither did he allow the strength of the passions, as he assessed them, to overturn the benevolent scheme of the universe as a whole. The reconciliation of dominant passions with a benevolent creation is one of Pope's most significant steps toward a final vindication of God.

At the simplest level Pope's vindication of the passions is aimed at a notion that was commonly labeled Stoicism. In fact, much of the total content of the moral reflections of the Stoic philosophers had become party-line Christianity, and, except for two ideas associated with them, Stoics were admired by Pope's contemporaries; but those two ideas, to many minds, constituted what the age called Stoicism. The one idea (their supposed fatalism) is of no concern to the immediate discussion. The other was clearly the concept most frequently conjured up by the word *Stoicism*. This was the idea that virtue demands of man a complete suppression of the passions. Pope's contemporaries were virtually unanimous in concluding that the Stoic attitude toward the passions was a result of pride. The Stoics overlooked the fact that the passions are a vital part of the creature man. Contemporary thought agreed that reason cannot obliterate the passions, but it must regulate them. Though this conclusion was nearly universal, the frequent references to the pride of the Stoic attitude toward the passions testify that the Stoic notions were regarded as alive and in need of combating. The English translation of Antoine Le Grand's *Man Without Passion: or the Wise Stoick* was published as late as 1675. Probably more important, translations of the great Stoic writers, especially Marcus Aurelius, appeared regularly. The introductory essays and glosses of the translations dutifully supplied refutations of the onerous notions regarding passions. Le Grand gives the basic position of the Stoics in a fairly modern statement.

A wise man must as well be without *Passions* as free from Vices, and exempt from that which may render him miserable, as from that which may make him guilty. If small offences disturb his Conscience, *Passions*, how much soever moderated, interrupt his rest. . . . So that as to be Judg of a sound body all infirmities must be removed from it, likewise all *Passions* must be banisht from the Soul to make Judgment of her Tranquillity.[1]

Pope's attitude toward the passions is founded on a rejection of the Stoic notion and in that is commonplace, but the usual refutation of Stoicism still gives to reason the power to control if not suppress the passions. Pope does this too, but in a rather unusual way. The usual proposition, that reason is man's ruling characteristic, Pope rejects. In his system the split in man's nature is not between reason and the passions, per se, but between reason and self-love, a concentrated, pervasive, and general force of which the individual passions are modes. Of primary significance, Pope, by logical necessity, makes the predominant motivation of man to be self-love. He makes of reason a tool to be used for attaining those ends dictated by self-love. Reason, that is, helps self-love to select ends appropriate to its actual needs. Reason, therefore, is supposed to moderate the passions, but it moderates them so that they will accord with the enlightened ends of self-love, not in order that they may harmonize with an abstract perception of virtue. Because of this evaluation of reason, much of what Pope says about the passions is addressed to their combined existence in self-love.

In asserting that the passions are modes of self-love Pope is denying himself access to one important way in which the passions were sometimes vindicated by his contemporaries. Joseph Butler attempted to provide a satisfactory adjustment of the relationship between self-love, the passions, and virtue in response to Shaftesbury's denial that self-love and virtue can coexist. Butler was not prepared to grant that either reason or self-love existed in the extreme and dominant state that some

1. Anthony Le Grand, *Man Without Passions: or, the Wise Stoick, according to the Sentiments of Seneca*, trans. G. R. (London, 1675), pp. 105–6.

writers described. The position that he arrives at is a compromise. In his sermon "Upon the Love of Our Neighbor" Butler defends the compatibility of self-love and benevolence by showing self-love to be just *one* of the passions, with proper objects for its fulfillment, as the other passions have proper objects for theirs. (He suggests that self-love is everyone's favorite passion.)

Every man hath a general desire of his own happiness; and likewise a variety of particular affections, passions, and appetites to particular external objects. The former proceeds from, or is self-love; and seems inseparable from all sensible creatures, who can reflect upon themselves and their own interest or happiness, so as to have that interest an object to their minds: what is to be said of the latter is, that they proceed from, or together make up that particular nature, according to which man is made. The object the former pursues is somewhat internal, our own happiness, enjoyment, satisfaction; whether we have, or have not, a distinct particular perception what it is, or wherein it consists: the objects of the latter are this or that particular external thing, which the affections tend towards, and of which it hath always a particular idea or perception. The principle we call self-love never seeks anything external for the sake of the thing, but only as a means of happiness or good: particular affections rest in the external things themselves. One belongs to a man as a reasonable creature reflecting upon his own interest or happiness. The other, though quite distinct from reason, are as much a part of human nature.[2]

The goal, or proper object, pursued by self-love is happiness. Each of the other passions has its proper fulfillment as well. There may be a sense in which Butler's distinction is semantic, for he admits that self-love spurs men on to the fulfillment of any of their passions. That is to say, there is possibly some degree to which every passion has motivating force because of the happiness its fulfillment provides. But that degree, Butler insists, is not so considerable as to take over the claim to motivation. If one has a passion for food, what he aims at is the eating of the food itself. It is absurd to say that one eats because

2. Butler, pp. 138–39.

he wishes to be happy; he eats because he is hungry, though there may be some degree to which he is moved not to be hungry because hunger would prevent his being happy. Self-love is a passion that seeks a state of mind called *happiness*. Butler insists that self-love, when it acts in a secondary or mediate manner (such as with hunger), must not be mistaken for the immediate satisfaction that every passion seeks. His purpose in this argument is to show that benevolence and self-love are compatible. In order to accomplish this juggling of motives, he posits a passion for the good of others quite separate from the passion for happiness that is self-love. In this way, since self-love derives happiness from the gratification of the other passions, self-love may be pleased by benevolence. This does not mean for Butler that benevolence is selfish, for it has its own ends quite apart from what it may contribute to the fulfillment of self-love.

Happiness consists in the gratification of certain affections, appetites, passions, with objects which are by nature adapted to them. Self-love may indeed set us on work to gratify these: but happiness or enjoyment has no immediate connexion with self-love, but arises from such gratification alone. Love of our neighbor is one of those affections.[3]

Butler is attempting to reach a clarification of motives by showing that the number of passions should be enlarged rather than contracted. Other positions (such as an attempt to narrow all passions to the singular force of self-love) are, he feels, an oversimplification of the complexities of human motivation. Even the notion that self-love and social love are the same is effectively denied by Butler's conclusion; as he assesses motivation, social love is one of the passions and, as such, may fulfill self-love by attaining its proper goal. Self-love, then, can be gratified by the success of the strivings of social love just as it is by the success of any of the other passions. To Butler, this inter-

3. Ibid., pp. 147–48.

play does not mean that self-love and social love are the same but only that one can affect the other.

The foundation of Butler's distinction is that the passions other than self-love pursue the objects of their desire for the sake of the thing itself. This is proven by the fact that the passions frequently lead men after objects detrimental to their actual good. Men cannot, therefore, be motivated entirely by self-love, or they could never pursue what will hurt them. Butler distinguishes between

... the principle of an action, proceeding from cool consideration that it will be to my own advantage; and an action, suppose of revenge, or of friendship, by which a man runs upon certain ruin, to do evil or good to another. It is manifest the principles of these actions are totally different, and so want different words to be distinguished by: all that they agree in is, that they both proceed from, and are done to gratify an inclination in a man's self. But the principle or inclination in one case is self-love; in the other, hatred or love of another. There is then a distinction between the cool principle of self-love, or general desire of our happiness, as one part of our nature, and one principle of action; and the particular affections towards particular external objects, as another part of our nature, and another principle of action. How much soever therefore is to be allowed to self-love, yet it cannot be allowed to be the whole of our inward constitution; because you see, there are other parts or principles which come into it.[4]

One might object, however, that self-love never moves toward an object unless pleasure is anticipated as a result of the movement, though sometimes self-love may make a mistake. Pope defines the passions as modes of self-love because he asserts that men always intend to satisfy themselves when they pursue anything. To Pope, that is, man always intends that an action will contribute to his happiness. Reason's employment is to distinguish between what will and what will not contribute to a man's happiness.

4. Ibid., pp. 139–40.

Butler's position is somewhat nearer Pope's than the opposite extreme of Shaftesbury's moral sense and abstract devotion to the welfare of others, but Butler does not share Pope's willingness to grant the conclusion that all action is reducible to self-love. Butler's "cool principle of self-love" contrasts with Pope's combination of reason and self-love in which the cool, deliberative member is reason. To Pope, it seems, self-love has no capacity for being cool and can be restrained only by warnings of danger, immediate or eventual. Self-love is given whatever enlightenment it has by its association with reason. Self-love is a principle that would of itself "flame lawless thro' the void" (II, 65), and that is precisely the quality Butler denies in his logical distinction. Pope, however, denies Butler's insistence that self-love would never do anything to hurt itself when he asserts that self-love does not know what will hurt it and what will not and consequently must seek the counsel of reason.

Pope's General Defense of the Passions

The core of Pope's system for assessing and dealing with the passions is contained in five assertions.[5] (1) The passions, no

5. (1) Passions, like Elements, tho' born to fight,
    Yet, mix'd and soften'd, in his work unite:
    These 'tis enough to temper and employ;
    But what composes Man, can Man destroy?
               (II, 111–14)
The necessity for self-love would also apply to the passions:
    Self-love, the spring of motion, acts the soul;
    Reason's comparing balance rules the whole.
    Man, but for that, no action could attend,
    And, but for this, were active to no end;
    Fix'd like a plant on his peculiar spot,
    To draw nutrition, propagate, and rot;
    Or, meteor-like, flame lawless thro' the void,
    Destroying others, by himself destroy'd.
               (II, 59–64)
(2) Passions, like Elements, tho' born to fight
    Yet, mix'd and soften'd in his work unite. . . .
               (II, 111–12)
(3) The surest Virtues thus from Passions shoot. . . .
               (II, 183)

matter what objections may be made to them, are necessary in such a creature as man. (2) They do, however, have a potential danger which must be avoided. (3) On the other hand, they may lead to good as well as to ill. (4) Reason has the responsibility for furnishing man with the information to direct a proper choice among the passions. (5) Reason is finally weaker than self-love and, consequently, the passions.

The attempt to defend the passions by pointing out that they are necessary was usually intended to answer real or imaginary Stoic adversaries, though to different anti-Stoics there were different reasons for the necessity of the passions. Pope takes the ancient axiom that life demands motion[6] and adds to it the notion that the passions are responsible for motion in the human being, so that syllogistically the passions are necessary to life. Thus far the idea is commonplace and is based on the belief that reason is naturally resistant to motion. *Spectator* 408 gives a popular statement of the idea.

> The Understanding being of its self too slow and lazy to exert it self into Action, it's necessary it should be put in Motion by the gentle Gales of the Passions, which may preserve it from stagnating and Corruption; for they are as necessary to the Health of the Mind, as

---

(This is in a context dealing with the ruling passion.)

(4) Suffice that Reason keep to Nature's road,
    Subject, compound them [passions], follow her and God.
             (II, 115–16)

(5) Most strength the moving principle requires;
    Active its task, it prompts, impels, inspires.
    Sedate and quiet the comparing lies,
    Form'd but to check, delib'rate, and advise.
             (II, 67–70)

6. Cf. Hobbes, *Leviathan,* ch. 6: "For there is no such thing as perpetuall Tranquility of mind, while we live here; because Life it selfe is but Motion, and can never be without Desire, nor without Feare, no more than without Sense." John Bulwer, *Pathomyatomia or a Dissection of the Significative Muscles of the Affections of the Minde* (London, 1649), p. 1: "Motion, saith the Stagerite, is *Perfectio perfectibilis,* the perfection of that which is perfectible. 'Tis *ultima perfectio Creaturae,* Saith the Pergamite; The highest perfection of a Creature; for, a living creature, is a living Creature by moving. . . ."

the Circulation of the animal Spirits is to the Health of the Body; they keep it in Life, and Strength, and Vigour; nor is it possible for the Mind to perform its Offices without their Assistance: These Motions are given us with our Being, they are little Spirits that are born and dye with us; to some they are mild, easie, and gentle, to others wayward and unruly, yet never too strong for the Reins of Reason and the Guidance of Judgment.

To those who defined self-love as self-preservation, the passions become necessary in a more active way. If the organism were not strongly moved toward some things and away from others, it would be killed or die. Archbishop King defends the passions from this point of view.

God could have avoided all this by ordering that the Soul should not be affected by the Motions of the Body; or at least, that every thing done therein should be agreeable: But how dangerous this would be to Animals, any one may understand, who recollects how very short their Lives must be, if they died with the same Pleasure that they eat or drink or propagate their Species. . . . We must then either have been arm'd with these Passions against Death, or soon have perish'd. . . .[7]

In addition to these more biological defenses of the passions, one often encounters a moral defense. The passions are productive of good as well as evil. In order to secure good, men had to be motivated toward it; had the motivation in the form of passions been omitted, the creation would have lacked that amount of good. Since there was also quite general agreement that the passions are dangerous, this latter position is similar to one of Pope's ways of justifying the passions: they are neither good nor evil of themselves but may go in either direction, depending on the individual guidance they receive. Pope makes this defense of the passions explicit in lines 181–94 of the second epistle where he is talking of grafting a best principle on the ruling passion. He cites the kinship of spleen with honesty

7. King, p. 115. See also the following: Reynolds, pp. 46f.; Bulwer, pp. 2f; Thomas Chubb, "A Vindication of God's Moral Character," *A Collection of Tracts on Various Subjects* (London, 1730), p. 268.

or wit; sloth with philosophy; lust with love; envy with emulation; and ends with the following couplet:

> **Nor Virtue, male or female, can we name,**
> **But what will grow on Pride, or grow on Shame.**[8]

Generally, the idea that the passions lead to virtue does not of itself make sufficiently individualized demands on its context to allow a contrast between the way Pope manipulates this idea and the uses to which it is put by other writers. It is another malleable commonplace that can easily be used in a variety of contexts without altering them very noticeably or being altered by them very drastically. Pope's system is different in important ways from several others of which the idea forms a part, but the idea itself involves no important issue.

To summarize, the necessity of the passions was defended by Pope's contemporaries for reasons both physical and moral. A writer who admits the necessity of the passions for man acknowledges a basic element in man other than the spiritual; there was, however, little disagreement that man is necessarily a creature of both passion and reason. The issue was the predominance in man's nature of one or the other. The position already noticed in Wollaston grants the necessity of both reason and the passions but asserts the necessary predominance of reason.[9] The extreme opposite this position which puts reason in a position of inferior strength has already been noticed in John Clarke of Hull, Daniel Waterland, and, even more ex-

---

8. This couplet strongly suggests Mandeville's description of pride and shame as sources of what are called virtuous actions.

9. For examples see the following: John Ball, *The Power of Godliness* (London, 1675), p. 194; Tillotson, 2:641; George Burghope, *Autarchy: or, The Art of Self-Government* (London, 1691), p. 23; Francis Bragge, *A Practical Treatise of the Regulation of the Passions* (London, 1708), pp. 9–10; Reynolds, p. 43; Walter Charleton, *Natural History of the Passions* (London, 1671), sig. A3rf; Marin Cureau de la Chambre, *The Art How to Know Men*, trans. John Davies (London, 1665), p. 175; William Ayloffe, *The Government of the Passions* (London, 1700), p. 12; Humphry Ditton, *A Discourse Concerning the Resurrection of Jesus Christ* (London, 1712), p. 520–21.

tremely, in Mandeville and Hobbes. Pope is close to Mandeville in his purpose of mortifying man's pride, and to some extent the dominance of the passions in his system aids in the mortification, but he turns the conclusion in quite a different direction by adjusting the definition of virtue and relying on a benevolent system that is not dependent on man's intention for its excellence.

Restraining the Passions

Hand in hand with the attempt to justify the passions went the realization that there was also a danger in trying to justify them too far, for despite their necessity and their good qualities, the passions, as many writers recognized, were potentially dangerous and had in some way to be kept under control or within bounds.[10] The stronger the passions, however, the more difficult the job of restraining them; different writers envisioned different ways in which the job might be done. The most pious answer referred the passions to the control of grace but, beyond that uncontrollable force, the general view was that reason was responsible for restraining the passions.[11]

The position that reason must in some way temper or adjust the passions usually carries with it, at least by implication, the idea of the superiority of reason and the baseness of the passions. There is at least a hint of disdain in Pope's handling of the passions, and there is also a suggestion of an exaltation of reason, but Pope differs substantially from other writers who make the same evaluations of reason and the passions as they speak of the guiding forces in man. One group of writers, for example, asserts that while reason and the passions were once

10. For some varied warnings against the dangers of the passions, see the following: Thomas Wright, *Of the Passions of the Mind in General* (London, 1601), pp. 88–89; Reynolds, p. 65; Jean-Francois Senault, *The Use of the Passions*, trans. Henry, Earl of Monmouth (London, 1671), p. 105; David Papillon, *The Vanity of the Lives and Passions of Men* (London, 1651), p. 131; Wollaston, pp. 316–17; Chubb, p. 254.

11. Reynolds, p. 60; Senault, p. 119; Ball, p. 177; *Spectator*, No. 408; Wollaston, pp. 325–26.

in proper balance (that is, they were naturally so), this natural balance was upset by the Fall. As a result of the Fall, reason and the passions have become antagonistic to one another.[12] Pope does not rely on the distinction between man as he was created and man as he is found in a corrupted state (the distinction is not relevant to a system of natural religion). He describes what he considers to be a necessary relationship, not a corrupted one, when he speaks of reason as less strong than self-love. Other writers base their vindication of man as he is, that is in a fallen state, on the notion that reason is the stronger of the two parts of human nature.

Even when there was agreement that reason is responsible for keeping the passions under control, the notions governing the dictum may have been different. The most pressing issue arose when an author gave his theory of how reason accomplishes the task it is assigned. To Pope the guides at the disposal of reason as it attempts to keep the creature within the bounds of true self-love are pleasure and pain, nature, and conscience (plus, to a lesser extent, utility). If, for Pope, man were corrupted in the sense that many sermonizing divines understood in defining corruption, reason would have no chance of performing its job satisfactorily because that corruption itself would be an aberration from man's real, original nature. A man who has become genuinely unnatural can only be saved by a superior outside force. No appeal to a corrupted nature would be effective. Pope recognizes the weakness of reason, but, as he describes it, the weakness of reason in relation to self-love is justifiable in terms of the whole system in which it operates, for the system is as it should be. Reason is, then, finally left with the assistance of the guides inherent in nature as it guards the individual; but, for Pope, reason is a kind of guard different from the sort described by other defenders of reason.

Many writers of this period agree that reason must temper and not destroy the passions, but they appear to think of reason

12. Senault, p. 155; Reynolds, p. 61; Papillon, sig. A3r.

as some sort of relatively abstract capacity able to distinguish good from bad and to seek its own choice. They nearly equate reason with man as a distinguishable species. Reason is to them the commanding characteristic which tells man what he is. It constitutes man's essential nature. To them, a man's reason is nearly the man; but, to Pope, reason is a tool. A complex and uncertain self uses the tool to attain its ends.[13]

The French clergyman Jean-Francois Senault, for example, uses the familiar metaphor of the passions and the sea to show the power of reason in ruling the creature.

Since our good fortune is in our own power, and that we sail upon a Sea, the calm or tempest whereof depends upon our will; we may shun the Rocks the Sea hides, asswage the fury of the winds which make it go high, bring low the waves which it raiseth, and make a calm succeed a storm; or by a more lucky application, we may make those Rocks hide their heads, those Seas to bear our Vessels, and those winds to conduct them.[14]

The quotation is taken from Senault's fourth discourse, "That in what condition soever our Passions be, they may be governed by Reason." Reason is clearly put in the position of subduing the passions by the use of principles essentially reasonable. There are several similarities between Pope's and Senault's ideas in this quotation; of particular importance, both cite the necessity for reason to exert some controlling influence over the storms of the passions.

In Pope's thinking, however, the predominant characteristic of man is self-love which is embodied in the passions. There is no reason to conclude that Pope is positing any power in reason

13. It is particularly interesting to notice that this point of view has strong Scriblerian connections. R. S. Crane argues most convincingly that the fourth book of *Gulliver's Travels* is a satiric denial of the conventional definition of man as a rational animal ("The Houyhnhnms, the Yahoos, and the History of Ideas," in *Reason and the Imagination: Studies in the History of Ideas, 1600–1800,* ed. Joseph A. Mazzeo [New York, 1962]). Pope's view of man as dominated by self-love and the passions rather than reason seems kindred.

14. Senault, p. 115.

to make self-love submit to the qualities of abstract reasonableness, just as he does not describe man in pursuit of abstract virtue or benevolence. For Pope reason controls the passions by finding out the path of enlightened self-love. Other writers, in varying degrees, insist that reason forces the passions to submit to the power of logical observation or to the truths inherent in natural relationships abstracted from personal benefit. In Pope's system reason does not steer or command but provides the information by which steering and commanding are done.[15]

Although Pope touches upon moderation as another sort of ethical guide, it plays a rather curious part in his system. Neither Pope nor any of his contemporaries would be found counseling against moderation; there is, therefore, no issue to be found on that subject. On the other hand, a system which approves a ruling passion is certainly not in harmony with the sort of recommendation of moderation that one would usually find. Pope recommends a tempering and softening of the passions.

> Passions, like Elements, tho' born to fight,
> Yet, mix'd and soften'd, in his work unite:
> These 'tis enough to temper and employ;
> But what composes Man, can Man destroy?
>
> . . . .
> These mix'd with art, and to due bounds confin'd,
> Make and maintain the balance of the mind. . . .
>   (II, 111–20)

This quotation is a reply to Stoic approval of the suppression of all passion, but "due bounds" is sufficiently ambiguous to allow a wide variety of actual functioning in the passions, since *due* would be determined by the needs of the system rather than by a universal rule that no passion must exceed a certain specific degree of expression. Even a predominant passion would be within the "due bounds" since Pope defends the necessity of a predominant passion to give unity to every man's endeavors.

15. See note 17 below for a fuller explication of reason as the card.

Presumably, "due bounds" would also recognize that every passion must urge with sufficient force to move the creature into action.

Pope's position (since "Reason's comparing balance rules the whole" [II, 60]) is that reason's responsibility is to see that a balance suitable to the needs of the whole is maintained. Presumably reason does not moderate the passions for the sake of moderation but to protect the whole against the ravaging encroachments of single passions. The ruling passion "swallows up the rest," but this probably means that other passions express themselves in a direction dictated by the ruling passion rather than that they receive no fulfillment at all. There is in Pope's ideas about the ruling passion an awareness of its danger; he calls it "the Mind's disease" (II, 138) and "our vice" (II, 196), but he still approves it and recognizes the need for immoderate motivation to keep the world going in a purposeful direction.

In final summary, the contrast between Pope's assertions about reason and those of many of his contemporaries is made especially clear in their varying uses of the commonplace comparison of the passions to winds and a man's life to the movement of a ship. To Senault, whose use of the metaphor was quoted above, the passions are like the elements. We have it in our control to govern the elements so that they do not disturb us any more than we want them to or is appropriate.

Spectator No. 408 differs from Senault and takes a step nearer Pope:

Reason must be employed in adjusting the Passions, but they must ever remain the Principles of Action.

The strange and absurd Variety that is so apparent in Mens Actions, shews plainly they can never proceed immediately from Reason; so pure a Fountain emits no such troubled Waters: They must necessarily arise from the Passions, which are to the Mind as the Winds to a Ship, they only can move it, and they too often destroy it; if fair and gentle they guide it into the Harbour, if contrary and furious they overset it in the Waves: In the same Manner is the

Mind assisted or endangered by the Passions; Reason must then take the Place of Pilot, and can never fail of securing her Charge if she be not wanting to her self: The Strength of the Passions will never be accepted as an Excuse for complying with them; they were designed for Subjection, and if a Man suffers them to get the upper Hand, he then betrays the Liberty of his own Soul.

Spectator No. 408 bears such strong resemblances to Pope's thoughts concerning the passions that it has, on internal evidence, been attributed to him.[16] It says nearly everything Pope says about the necessary interaction between reason and the passions. There is one difference, however, and it stems from a significantly different conclusion about man's reason. *Spectator* No. 408 says that reason must be the pilot, and Pope calls reason the card, that is the compass.[17]

> The rising tempest puts in act the soul,
> Parts it may ravage, but preserves the whole.
> On life's vast ocean diversely we sail,
> Reason the card, but Passion is the gale;
> Nor God alone in the still calm we find,
> He mounts the storm, and walks upon the wind.
> (II, 105–10)

16. See Donald F. Bond, "Pope's Contributions to the *Spectator*," *Modern Language Quarterly* 5 (1944): 69–70. Bond considers the ascription doubtful.

17. The Elwin-Courthope edition of the works of Pope gives the following identification of *card*: "In the mariner's compass the paper on which the points of the compass are marked is called 'the card' " (2:384). That Pope meant the compass as a whole rather than the card separately is suggested by the following manuscript lines cited in Elwin-Courthope on the authority of Warburton's edition. These lines follow "reason the card, but passion is the gale":

> A tedious voyage! where how useless lies
> The compass, if no pow'rful gusts arise!

A compass is an appropriate metaphor for Pope's concept of reason because the compass is not an inert repository of information such as a map but an instrument that uses the forces in the world to enable it to tell which direction is which; its value depends on an owner who knows where he is going and needs helpful and accurate information to enable him to get there.

There is some trouble with the metaphor of reason as the pilot, especially when it must adjust the winds and subject them. Pope's metaphor avoids that difficulty. To him reason is used to determine how desires may be accomplished; it does not supply the desires itself. It is a passive principle in the sense that it is *used;* but it still moves its observation and attention to examine fully the characteristics of the world outside. Reason does not provide motivation; it finds out ways to accomplish the motivation provided by the passions and predicts the outcome of individual actions so that self-love will have an accurate awareness of what will reward it and what will not. Probably the soul is the pilot in this metaphor. The passions, as winds, propel the ship, and reason tells the soul in what direction its desired destination lies so that the soul may adjust the course of the whole creature to the winds in order to attain its chosen port. Reason does not choose the port (presumably happiness or the fulfillment of self-love), nor does it steer the ship. It also does not regulate the winds. As the quotation continues, however, Pope demonstrates that he sees the need for accomplishing all these tasks.

> Passions, like Elements, tho' born to fight,
> Yet, mix'd and soften'd, in his work unite:
> These 'tis enough to temper and employ;
> But what composes Man, can Man destroy?
> Suffice that Reason keep to Nature's road,
> Subject, compound them, follow her and God.
>
> (II, 111–16)

The passions, then, are mixed and softened, though, strictly speaking, the quotation does not say that reason does this. Reason subjects and compounds the passions. Reason rules the whole. Passions, that is, must be adjusted so that the needs of the whole creature are not frustrated, and, if one is to take Pope literally, presumably reason is responsible for showing how various combinations will work, and enlightened self-love will choose according to the information it has received. The winds of the passions will be tempered by following nature because self-love will not let the passions loose if it knows they will be destructive. The most important facet of this metaphor is that reason is a tool in the hands of the whole creature, a tool for telling how to get where it is going. The metaphor is different from one in which reason can exert its effect on the basis of what it thinks, by its own abstractions, the destination should be.

6

The Ruling Passion

There would apparently have been little disagreement between Pope and most of his contemporaries on the subject of the passions except for Pope's assertion that they are, and must be, stronger than reason. That conclusion on Pope's part carries with it an assessment of man altered from that of many of his contemporaries since it makes man predominantly a passionate creature, with reason serving a specific function, rather than a creature predominantly reasonable.

Pope follows a similar path in reaching a somewhat more startling conclusion, that men are guided by a ruling passion.

Two steps may be recalled. Men conclude that the world is faulty because they do not see the whole and because they are not aware that the structure of all the parts is a result of the relationship of each part to the entire structure. In other words, there is a predominant purpose in the world (order), dictated by a predominant attribute of the creator (wisdom); once this is known, the parts can be understood more accurately because the principle from which their existence stems is clear. Then too, because men are living creatures and must have the motion necessary to life, they must have passions to move them. They have *ruling* passions because they are parts of a larger organized structure and must have a motivation that will fulfill whatever purpose they accomplish for that structure. Otherwise they would operate at random from mere personal caprice.

As Pope defends God's creation from charges of inaccuracy by an appeal to overall purpose, so he defends man from a charge of aimlessness by positing in him an all-encompassing motivation which other passions serve and advance. That this latter is the function of the ruling passion is clearer from "Epistle I. To Richard Temple, Viscount Cobham" than from the *Essay on Man*.[1] In the former poem Pope specifically asks why men are capricious and answers that they *seem* so because the viewer is unaware of the existence of a ruling passion; once the ruling passion is seen, apparent caprice falls into an intelligible pattern, and a man no longer stands incapable of coherent explanation.

In Pope's system the ruling passion presents the same obvious danger that any passions do that are stronger than reason. Such passions may take control and result in destruction more dangerous than the lassitude they are intended to overcome. The actual dangers of both the passions and the ruling passion are tempered because man's psychological structure is included in a system arranged so that the fulfillment of his ultimate physi-

---

1. The Cobham epistle ("*Of the* Knowledge *and* Characters *of* Men") and the fourth epistle of the *Essay* were both published in January 1733/4. The first three epistles of the essay were published from February to May, 1733.

cal and moral purposes is not dependent upon his intention to do what the world requires but is a result of superior operations over which he has no control and into which he has little insight.

Pope's use of the ruling passion, then, stands in direct opposition to two formidable structures of thought involving the passions. In the one the passions must be moderate and under the domination of reason in order to be acceptable, and in the other man is an absurd, immoral, or amoral creature, victim of whatever trivial impulses happen to attract his attention.

Pope's assertion that a master passion exists and gives concentration and direction to the creature is quite simple and direct. The senses perceive objects outside the man, and he is attracted to or repelled by the objects as a result of what he sees in them. (This attraction or repulsion is a loose definition of a passion.) These passions are constantly present to human consciousness.

> Pleasures are ever in our hands or eyes,
> And when in act they cease, in prospect rise;
> Present to grasp, and future still to find,
> The whole employ of body and of mind.
> (II, 123–26)

While all of a man's sense experiences have some power to attract, all do not attract equally strongly because each man has organs, and thus sensitivities, of varying strength. One man is more sensitive to some experiences than to others, and the ones he feels particularly strongly are most potent to move him. The strongest attraction (which is to say the most sensitive "organ of the frame") becomes the dominant force in the personality, swallowing up others in its thirst to be satisfied.

> All spread their charms, but charm not all alike;
> On diff'rent senses diff'rent objects strike;
> Hence diff'rent Passions more or less inflame,
> As strong or weak, the organs of the frame;
> And hence one master Passion in the breast,
> Like Aaron's serpent, swallows up the rest.
> (II, 127–32)

Pope then goes on to describe the danger of the ruling passion (he calls it the "Mind's disease" and "peccant part"). It may gain excessive sway over reason. He finally resolves the difficulty by defending the passion as useful and necessary. He argues that reason need only act as a guard (presumably as it proceeds about its main business, distinguishing between real and illusory good).

> Yes, Nature's road must ever be prefer'd;
> Reason is here no guide, but still a guard:
> 'Tis hers to rectify, not overthrow,
> And treat this passion more as friend than foe:
> A mightier Pow'r the strong direction sends,
> And sev'ral Men impels to sev'ral ends.
> Like varying winds, by other passions tost,
> This drives them constant to a certain coast.
> Let pow'r or knowledge, gold or glory, please,
> Or (oft more strong than all) the love of ease;
> Thro' life 'tis followed, ev'n at life's expence;
> The merchant's toil, the sage's indolence,
> The monk's humility, the hero's pride,
> All, all alike, find Reason on their side.
>
> (II, 161–74)

The final step in the vindication of the ruling passion is the mysterious inclusion of a predominant virtue grafted to it. The frequently expressed defense of the lesser passions, that they move men forcefully toward good, appears closely related to this inclusion of a master virtue.

> Th' Eternal Art educing good from ill,
> Grafts on this Passion our best principle:
> 'Tis thus the Mercury of Man is fix'd,
> Strong grows the Virtue with his nature mix'd;
> The dross cements what else were too refin'd,
> And in one interest body acts with mind.
> As fruits ungrateful to the planter's care
> On savage stocks inserted learn to bear;
> The surest Virtues thus from Passions shoot,
> Wild Nature's vigor working at the root.
>
> (II, 175–84)

In thus relating virtue to an inborn quality placed in man by
the creator of the whole (the idea may have some relation to
Butler's natural affections toward good objects), Pope adds a
major point to his humbling of man's pride by making the
virtue of which men are capable dependent not on men themselves but on God and nature instead.

> **Thus Nature gives us (let it check our pride)**
> **The virtue nearest to our vice ally'd;**
> **Reason the byass turns to good from ill,**
> **And Nero reigns a Titus, if he will.**
>
> (II, 195–98)

The last line of this quotation may give some insight into one
aspect of Pope's thought upon which he lays little stress, that
is, his idea of free will. For, even with the makeup of the individual man so carefully planned by his creator, "Nero reigns
a Titus, if he will."

In order to put Pope's group of ideas about the existence of
a ruling passion into proper perspective, one needs to see the
assertion that men are ruled by one predominant motivation in
its simplest form. Basically the assertion is that out of the multi-
ple motives and drives that determine a human being's actions,
one motivation may gain sufficient control to become predominant over the others. For the moment it will be valuable
to consider this one drive as either permanent or temporary;
the main problem is its existence and the attitude various writers had toward a single passion predominating in a man's
activities.

Senault can be put at one end of a range of writers positing
the existence of a ruling passion. His concept of the passion
which "bears most sway" is not organized to represent a fully
distinguishable and separate part of the individual's nature in
the sense that Pope's master passion is such a part, but in a
rather general way the two ideas can be considered together.
For Senault the passions need to be kept in balance, and any
deviation from the natural balance would represent an evil
and an abuse. One function of reason is to see that the balance

is maintained. Senault's master passion, then, has gotten out of balance, and it robs some others of their own satisfaction. From the context, it is difficult to determine whether Senault is thinking of an overall ruling passion in the manner of Pope or whether he is referring to whatever passion is at the moment in the position of mastery (though the latter seems more likely); however, his reference to the passion "which bears most sway" reflects an attitude toward the concept Pope uses, whether the passion is fixed or temporary.

> Sometimes also a man may set upon that particular Passion which bears most sway with him, that he may vanquish those that fight under the others Colours, and the Victory is had by one Blow; by the Generals death the whole Army is defeated.[2]

Senault's argument in this quotation shares with Pope the idea that a mastering passion swallows up others to use them for its own purposes. A bit later, however, Senault refers in more detail to the nature of the master passion and the necessity to deal with it sternly.

> One may very well sometimes oppose pleasure to grief, hope to fear, and inclination to aversion, but in this combate Reason must take heed, lest by weakening one Passion, she add too much strength unto another; and that whilst she would reduce a Mutinier to obedience, she do not augment the number of Rebels. When she undertakes these affairs, she must hold the Scales in her hand: and remember that God (whom she imitateth) doth all his Works by weight and measure; and when he tempers the qualities of the Elements, to the end that he may agree them, he doth no advantage to one whereby another is prejudiced. We may likewise well assail the Passion that masters us, and which we acknowledge to be the cause of our disorders: For it is a Familiar which possesseth us; 'tis a Tyrant which useth not his power, save in order to his own interest; and who is so much the more dangerous, as that he endeavors to become welcom. Reason is bound to oppugne him as a publick Enemy, and to employ all her might, if not to destroy him, at least to weaken him.[3]

2. Senault, p. 117.
3. Ibid., pp. 119–20.

The similarities of this long passage to Pope's ideas on the subject are evident. The master passion is a "familiar," and its power, because of its naturalness (Senault earlier notes that passions are born with us and grow as we grow), suggests a concept similar to Pope's. The difference is equally evident, for to Senault the passion mastering a man must be regarded as the enemy and brought into submission by reason, a conclusion exactly opposite Pope's warning to treat the passion "more as friend than foe." Perhaps the most basic difference between the concepts (for surely Pope admits the dangers of the ruling passion as overtly as Senault does) is that Senault's ideas are founded on the notion that a balance is necessary for a satisfactory state, while to Pope some strong urge must break the stasis or overcome the lassitude of a sluggish element (whether the subject be man or nature) for life and the movement essential to life. Therefore, Senault can be taken to represent at one extreme a negative attitude toward man's capacity to be dominated by one urgent drive at the expense of the fulfillment of all the motivations of the whole creature.

An Imbalance in the Humors

Pope's theory of the predominant passion undoubtedly stems from the observation that men are often powerfully motivated in a single, strong, if not monomaniacal, direction. One explanation of such a phenomenon was available from the age-old theories of a "humors" psychology. In humors theory the ideal (but not humanly attainable) condition of a man would be a perfect balance of the four humors and qualities, but the recognition was general that one quality or humor would predominate and give each man a certain kind of temperament or complexion. Various mixtures were also recognized so that there were usually nine types rather than four.

Instead of explaining the existence of ruling passions, the theory of the governing power of the humors apparently arrived at a description of what we would now call temperament. Humoral psychology described the governing mood or attitude rather than the governing passion. To be sure, one humor was supposed to be more amorous or martial or more studious than another, and within those loose bounds a humor could dictate a ruling passion, but the bounds were loose, and the more important part of the distinction was the manner of pursuing an object rather than the object pursued; even so sanguine a passion as love might be engaged in phlegmatically.

Literary Theory of the Humors

More important for immediate consideration is what might be called the literary theory of the humors. It is not essentially very different from the medical theory, on which it is based, but it is combined with an ethical attitude, and the ethical intention of Pope's poem also gives to his theory of the ruling passion an ethical direction. There is in most literary use of humors psychology a prescription for men's conduct of their affairs as well as a description of how men act.

For the literary theory of the humors one would obviously turn to Ben Jonson. His grounds for judging his characters are apparently similar to Senault's since Jonson's humors-characters are subjects of disapproval. The humors-character is a comic figure, an example of imbalance; he is purged and the balance reestablished during the play, or he is degraded and defeated.[4]

A more detailed account of Jonson's humors theory may be delayed for a page or two so that a few important philosophical implications of what has thus far been said about Jonson and Senault may be examined while their basic position is still fresh. In Jonson and Senault there is the fundamental assumption that goodness and virtue are to be found in equilibrium, a view common to their ages. To some of Pope's contemporaries such an evaluation of human life might be said to ignore the necessity for variety and order in society (*order* used in Pope's sense of *gradation*). Would it not be true, one might argue, that if all

4. Robert Van Akin Bauer, *The Use of Humors in Comedy by Ben Jonson and His Contemporaries* (Urbana, 1947), p. 6.

men were balanced mixtures of the humors or passions, all men would be alike? This objection either implies or assumes that some of the work of the world would not be done at all were men not violently motivated to do certain jobs; therefore, something other than equilibrium is necessary to diversity.

It should probably be noticed here that the ruling passion affects man primarily as a social creature rather than as a part of the great chain of being. A man functions at the level of the ruling passion *within* his link in the chain rather than *as* a link, since no one man is, strictly speaking, a link in the universe but only in his society. It is the *species* that is the link in the universal chain of being. I do not know that any of Pope's contemporaries ever made the distinction perfectly clear, but insofar as necessary order in the society and necessary order in the universe have a similarity, or are parallel, the similarity is general and metaphorical. While many writers would defend the necessity of the species man to the chain of creation, I am not aware that any writer ever attempted to defend the equal necessity of any one man to the fabric of society. The idea that there must be subordination in the society, that there must be a servant class as well as a ruling class, is an idea that was (it must be admitted) virtually taken for granted for nearly the whole century; and the idea bears an uncomfortable resemblance to the inevitability of the necessarily full chain that makes up the universe.

Sociologically-minded readers in the twentieth century are frequently rankled by the apparent indifference of eighteenth-century writers to the plight of the poor, an indifference that seems to be reflected in these two theories demonstrating the need for subordination (and for a similar reaction from within the eighteenth century one can turn to Samuel Johnson's review of Soame Jenyns' *Free Enquiry into the Nature and Origin of Evil*). In the practice of many writers, however (and Pope is among them), subordination in society and the necessary order of the great chain of being, while parallel, do not interact in such a way as to produce complacency in the face of the evils of the society. There is a seeming paradox in the fact that Pope could, in the *Essay on Man,* declare that "whatever is, is right" and also have produced *The Dunciad,* the *Epilogue to the Satires,* the "Epistle to Augustus" and others of his greatest poems, all of which are so filled with anger and indignation that they seem to say that esthetically, morally, and politically, whatever is, is wrong.

There is, however, no real paradox involved. Though he does not explicitly say it, Pope clearly did not hold that the inevitability of man's existence as man in the fabric of the universe meant that all social conditions were equally inevitable. Indeed, one of Pope's major purposes in the *Essay on Man* is the clarification of man's nature so that men will know what is within their power and what is not. With this knowledge they will not waste time and effort attempting what they cannot achieve or grieving over what they cannot change. They will be free to put all their efforts into those activities where it is possible to accomplish their ends. All of Pope's moral works proclaim that it is in his social existence (including moral and artistic activities) that man could, if he would, actually accomplish improvement.

There is another aspect of the controversy over man's moral control in relation to his physiological constitution which has implications for Pope's theory of the ruling passion. As Jonson and Senault establish morality or virtue in personally controlled equilibrium, they exalt the moral worth of man, making his virtue to be a product of his own actions, his own ability to control the forces within him. Fundamental to Pope's position is his intention to humble man's pride. One way of doing this is to diminish man's moral control (substituting self-love for reason as his dominant characteristic) and give the credit for morality and virtue in the world to God rather than man. There is no question that Pope attributes all to self-love: "Vice or Virtue, Self directs it still" (II, 236).

If, therefore, virtue exists, it exists because the universe is so arranged that what brings the individual man his pleasure

also brings pleasure to others (and vice versa). In a system
balanced in this manner, the personality governed by the imbalance of the ruling passion is not as destructive as it would
be if virtue were selflessness, for man is not capable of the
noble balance advised by Senault and admired by Jonson.
There is no need for him to be capable of this balance since the
universe is not arranged so as to need it. If these differences of
first principles be granted, an important difference between
the positions of Senault or Jonson and Pope becomes evident.
In the one, man is to some extent exalted by the evaluation that
gives him control over himself and puts the central responsibility for morality into his hands; in the other, man deserves
little credit, most of the effective virtue of the world devolving
to the responsibility and glory of God.

Since, however, there are some parallel concepts in the two
theories, Jonson's humors-morality needs further examination.
Much of the critical speculation about Jonson's theory of humors is based on the familiar passage from the induction to
Every Man Out of His Humour:

> Why, *Humour* (as 'tis *ens*) we thus define it
> To be a quality of aire or water,
> And in it selfe holds these two properties,
> Moisture, and Fluxure: As for demonstration,
> Poure water on this floore, 'twill wet and runne:
> Likewise the aire (forc't through a horne or trumpet)
> Flowes instantly away, and leaues behind
> A kind of dew; and hence we doe conclude,
> That what soe're hath fluxure, and humiditie,
> As wanting power to containe it selfe,
> Is *Humour.* So in euery humane body
> The choller, melancholy, flegme, and bloud,
> By reason that they flow continually
> In some one part, and are not continent,
> Receiue the name of Humours. Now thus farre
> It may, by *Metaphore,* apply it selfe
> Unto the generall disposition:
> As when some one peculiar quality

> Doth so possess a man, that it doth draw
> All his affects, his spirits, and his powers,
> In their confluctions, all to runne one way,
> This may be truly said to be a Humour.

There are three important things about this much of the definition. The first is that fundamental to the notion of humor is
the idea that it "wants power to contain itself." In other words,
the motion of a humor cannot be controlled. The second is that
Asper (the speaker, with whom Jonson is evidently sympathetic) limits the imbalance of a true humor to one of the four
humors (since they are the substances having the necessary
requisites for a real humor). The phrase "some one particular
quality" has usually been read to mean any drive or passion,
but the term is used twice in the quotation, and it seems likely
that the second use is in reference to the first. The term *quality*
had, in addition to its other meanings, a specific meaning in
humors psychology, the qualities being dry, moist, hot, and
cold. In the second line of the quotation the word is apparently
in reference to this specific meaning.[5] If this meaning is given
to the word in Asper's rather scientific discussion, the distinction between actual humors and slighter affectations is
clear.

The third point about this much of the quotation is that
Asper has nothing to say about a real humor, for, as he goes on,
the rest of his speech is about something different. It is about
those men who have eccentricities of a lighter and not really
compelling nature which they rationalize by calling them

5. The *OED* does not give this specialized meaning for the word *quality*,
but note the following: "The Elements be in number foure. Fire, Earth,
Ayre, and Water, and unto them are appendant so many qualities: Hot,
Cold, Moist, Dry . . ." (Levinus Lemnius, *The Touchstone of the Complexions*, trans. Thomas Newton [London, 1633] p. 40). "The erroneous
hypothesis of the four humors and four qualities might do well enough for
the delineation of general classes of passions and sufferings . . . ," (Hardin
Craig, ed., "Introduction," in Timothy Bright, *A Treatise of Melancholie*
[New York, 1940], p. vi [originally published in 1586]). See Ruth Leila
Anderson's *Elizabethan Psychology and Shakespeare's Plays* (Iowa City,
1927), pp. 30–36, for further quotations.

humors, presumably defending themselves in this way by allowing that they are in the grip of an uncontrollable force.[6] The passage continues:

> But that a rooke, in wearing a pyed feather,
> The cable hat-band, or the three-pild ruffe,
> A yard of shooetye, or the Switzers knot
> On his *French* garters, should affect a Humour!
> O, 'tis more then most ridiculous.
>   CORD. He speakes pure truth now, if an Idiot
> Have but an apish, or phantasticke straine,
> It is his Humour. ASP. Well I will scourge those apes;
> And to these courteous eyes oppose a mirrour,
> As large as is the stage, whereon we act:
> Where they shall see the times deformitie
> Anatomiz'd in euery nerue, and sinnew,
> With constant courage, and contempt of feare.

Asper's purpose is obviously didactic:

> And I will mixe with you in industrie
> To please, but whom? attentiue auditors,
> Such as will ioyne their profit with their pleasure,
> And come to feed their understanding parts. . . .

His purpose is to expose fools who defend their folly by calling it a humor, thus rationalizing that it is beyond their control. His attitude toward such rationalization is full of anger and scorn, and in lines 32–36, he makes the reason for his anger clear.

> And yet, not one of these but knowes his workes,
> Knows what damnation is, the deuill, and hell,
> Yet, hourely they persist, grow ranke in sinne,
> Puffing their soules away in perj'rous aire,
> To cherish their extortion, pride, or lusts.

---

6. "Though Jonson portrays, then, both the genuine and the affected humour, the humour of his comedy is almost exclusively affectation or eccentricity. . . . Jonson's definition, then, is really two-fold, embracing both the genuine and the affected or eccentric . . ." (Henry L. Snuggs, "The Comic Humours: A New Interpretation," *PMLA* 52 [1947]: 118–19).

On one level, then, one should apparently make a distinction between the characters in Jonson's play who ape humors to make their folly seem uncontrollable and men whose bodies are so constructed that they really have a humoral imbalance (and since Jonson is silent about the latter, perhaps he regards such men as beyond correction). Those who are carried away by passions not having the essential quality of a humor (its uncontrollability) are responsible for what they do. They are liable for punishment because they know what they are doing but do it anyway and as a consequence are involved in actual sin.[7]

The relationship of Jonson's humors psychology to Pope's ruling passion must remain vague because the word *humors* remains vague. Asper rails, to be sure, against the misuse of the word, but both he and the other characters in the play continue to use it to mean a slighter fault, and that meaning continued in literary use into Pope's time.[8] Important to the present

7. For a discussion of Jonson's moral position (but not a defense of the above interpretation of *quality*) see James D. Redwine, "Beyond Psychology: The Moral Basis of Jonson's Theory of Humour Characterization," *Journal of English Literary History* 28 (1961): 316–34. For one that is somewhat closer to the present discussion, see Snuggs.

8. "Humour is usually considered by critics, as a fainter or weaker habitual passion peculiar to comic characters, as being chiefly found in persons of lower degree than those proper for tragedy" (Ephraim Chambers, *Cyclopaedia*, "Humour"). ". . . By humour is meant some extravagant habit, passion, or affection, particular . . . to some one person, by the oddness of which, he is immediately distinguished from the rest of men" (John Dryden, "An Essay of Dramatic Poesy," *The Best of Dryden*, ed. Louis I. Bredvold [New York, 1933], p. 438). "I should be unwilling to venture even on a bare Description of *Humour*, much more, to make a Definition of it; but now my Hand is in, I will tell you what serves me instead of either. I take it to be, *A singular and unavoidable manner of doing or saying any thing, Peculiar and Natural to one Man only; by which his Speech and Actions are distinguished from those of other Men*" (William Congreve, "A Letter to Mr. Dennis concerning Humour in Comedy," *Works*, ed. Montague Summers [London, 1928], 3:165).

> A Humour is the Byass, of the Mind,
> By which with Violence, 'tis one way inclin'd:
> It makes our Actions lean on one side still;
> And in all Changes that way bends the Will

discussion is the moral attitude Jonson's theory maintains.[9]

The perspective gained by this interpretation of Jonson is important because of two things it accomplishes. The first is that it grants the possibility of humoral imbalance. This is a dangerous point; if a man is at the mercy of his humoral balance, where is personal responsibility, and where is free will? Secondly, however, free will is maintained and personal responsibility is retained because motivations other than actual temperamental construction are not regarded as beyond human control.

Neither Jonson nor Pope gives much stress to the danger that any theory of a predominant humor or predominant passion runs of psychological determinism. Pope's theory is probably the more severe of the two, yet he tells his reader that "Nero reigns a Titus, if he will." Both Pope and Jonson apparently decided that, despite humoral imbalance or a ruling passion, man has the freedom to exercise his natural capacities in a direction that is either good or bad, and he is free to choose the direction. Perhaps it would not be too strong to say that both writers hold men responsible for making the best use of what they are, and neither expects a man to change himself into something that he is not.

Although the above discussion is desirable as an illustration of how ethical and physical theories may combine and influence one another, the notion that Jonson's humors-character stands

---

(Thomas Shadwell, Epilogue to "The Humourists," *The Dramatic Works of Thomas Shadwell, Esq.*, 4 vols. [London, 1720], 1:213). The preface to the same play gives another definition: ". . . A Humour (being the Representation of some Extravagance of Mankind) cannot but in some thing resemble some Man or other, or it is monstrous and unnatural" (Ibid., p. 124). See also the preface to "The Virtuoso"): "Those slight circumstantial things mention'd before are not enough to make a good comical Humour; which ought to be such an Affectation, as misguides Men in Knowledge, Art, or Science, or that causes defection in Manners and Morality, or perverts their Minds in the Main Actions of their lives" (Ibid., p. 309).

9. For recognition of this moral view, see Redwine and his many references.

in relation to Pope's theory of the ruling passion as cause to effect is no very satisfactory way of conceiving the growth of ideas. What is really involved is two technical methods for explaining the same phenomenon. That men have some dominant interest or attitude or emotional cast has evidently been the observation of ages of history. How this predominance might come about is a question that has been given various answers at different times. While each succeeding theory might in some sense have grown out of its predecessor, it is equally true that each new theory is supposed to make the one that was held before obsolete; it is the intention of the theorist to supplant the older theory with a more accurate one.

A humoral imbalance was for many centuries an explanation for the observed differences in the motivations of men, but by Pope's time the physiological theory of the humors upon which Jonson built at least the outline of his structure was outmoded. It had been mortally wounded by Harvey. Humors were still mentioned in Pope's time, but seldom did anyone with even rudimentary knowledge of medicine mean blood, phlegm, choler, and melancholy by the term. All the vital bodily fluids were humors.[10] If Pope's theory of the ruling passion stands in

10. "... the Ancients made Four Humours in the Blood. ... But this Opinion is Cashiered, since the invention of the Circulation of the Blood. ... There are Three General Humours which work the whole Body, Blood, Lympha (a sort of pure Water) and the Nervous Juice; but there are several particular Humours, as Chyle, Bile, Spittle, Pancreatic Juice, Seed, &c." (Stephen Blancard, *The Physical Dictionary,* 2d ed. [London, 1693], "Humores" [note the ancients-and-moderns aspect of the controversy]). *"Former Ages were so prepossessed in favour of the* Ancients, *that they never apply'd themselves to learn any thing but what these had discovered.* Hippocrates *and* Galen *only were then studied.* They sought in all their Writings, *all that they were obliged to know to render them accomplished in their art. They imagin'd they knew all, and took those for* Visionaries, *who pretended to know more than these: And this is the reason they have been so extremely barren in their* Discoveries. *But, Thanks to the* Penetration *of an excellent* Philosopher *of this age,* it has been *discovered that the* Living Body *is only a* Machine. *Men have applied their Minds to discover its* Springs" (Dominique Beddevole, *Essays of Anatomy . . .,* 2d ed., trans. J. Scougall [London, 1696], sig. A5vf). See also: Peter Paxton, *Directory*

any relationship to the theory of humors, as this is based on physiology, it is as a rejection of that theory, for Pope's theory of motivation is based on differences in the organs of men rather than on humoral balance. Pope makes use of a newer theory to explain the old phenomenon of single-minded motivation.

There were available to Pope some literary discussions of characters dominated by single overwhelming passions, but these discussions should be applied to Pope cautiously. Dryden's discussion of character in the preface to *Troilus and Cressida* includes the following statement: "Yet it is still to be observed, that one virtue, vice, and passion, ought to be shown in every man, as predominant over all the rest."[11] Dryden's preface, however, is a work of literary theory rather than psychology, and the assertion that a character in a play ought to have a predominant passion is not equivalent to the assertion that every man does have one. Pope is using his theory (as the epistle to Cobham makes clear) to make sense out of and give continuity to our observations of the people we see in the world around us. Dryden's subject is not the same.

In his article on "Humour in the Age of Pope," Edward N. Hooker describes a shift in attitude toward a humors-character. Earlier such a character was a person to be chastised and ridiculed, but by Pope's time writers began to draw humors-characters as men representative of the genius of a nation who provide the variety necessary to fill out the social fabric. The positive evaluation of such characters is analogous to the insistence on the necessity of each link in the great chain of being because of its uniqueness as a link. Hooker says that Pope's

---

Physico-Medical (London, 1701, 1707), p. xvii; George Baglivi, *Practice of Physick*. . . . (London, 1704), p. 135. Nicholas Robinson, *A New System of the Spleen, Vapours, and Hypochondriack Melancholy . . .* (London, 1729), pp. 14–23; Gideon Harvey, *Discourse on the Vanities of Philosophy and Physic*, 3d ed. (London, 1702), sig. A3v; Robert James, *A Medicinal Dictionary* (London, 1743–45), "Humour," "Anatome."

11. Benjamin Boyce, *The Character-Sketches in Pope's Poems* (Durham, N. C., 1962), pp. 105–130. He uses Dryden, Mrs. Manley, Gully, and others.

ruling passion stems from this more general attitude.[12] The change in attitude towards unbalanced motivation in this period between Pope and Jonson has already been noted. In Jonson's evaluation, the admirable man was one in whom all the passions were balanced, but to Pope he was one in whom the necessarily ruling passion was directed toward a beneficent end. Along the way the Stoic view (for Jonson's morality is in this regard Stoic) was shown to be impractical because of the principle that, in order for a creature to move, a passion had to overcome his inertia. To that notion Pope adds another. In order for a man to move in a consistent and unified direction, a ruling passion has to direct his entire life.

Philosophical Attitudes toward the Ruling Passion

The Twickenham edition of the *Essay* gives quotations from Bacon and Montaigne which in a limited way show some similarity to Pope's use of the ideas that men have ruling passions and that they can be useful, but neither Bacon nor Montaigne does any more than mention the ruling passion.[13] Neither gives any clear indication of how he would define the term or how the drive would operate. One cannot, therefore, very satisfactorily compare their use of the ideas with Pope's.

On the other hand, a somewhat more important resemblance was noticed by Kenneth MacLean in his book *John Locke and English Literature of the Eighteenth Century*.[14] MacLean quotes

12. Edward N. Hooker, "Humour in the Age of Pope," *Huntington Library Quarterly* 11 (1948), 361–85. See also Stuart M. Tave, *The Amiable Humorist* (Chicago, 1960), ch. 5.

13. See Mack's discussion and the following: Bernard Mandeville, *The Fable of the Bees,* ed. F. B. Kaye (Oxford, 1924), 1:258; Shaftesbury, 2:26; Pierre Bayle, *Miscellaneous Reflections, Occasion'd by the Comet . . .* (London, 1708), p. 272; Jonathan Swift, "A Short Character of his Excellency Thomas Earl of Wharton," in *The Examiner and Other Pieces Written in 1710–11,* ed. Herbert Davis (Oxford, 1957), p. 180; and *Gulliver's Travels,* the Struldbrugg episode.

14. Kenneth MacLean, *John Locke and English Literature of the Eighteenth Century* (New Haven, 1936), pp. 45–48.

part of the following passage from *An Essay Concerning Human Understanding* as an indication that Locke came near positing a ruling passion in his essay. Locke, of course, denies the existence of innate ideas in men, but he admits the existence of some "innate practical principles."

Nature, I confess, has put into man a desire of happiness and an aversion to misery: these indeed are innate practical principles which (as practical principles ought) do continue constantly to operate and influence all our actions without ceasing; these may be observed in all persons and all ages, steady and universal; but these are inclinations of the appetite to good, not impressions of truth on the understanding. I deny not that there are natural tendencies imprinted on the minds of men, and that from the very first instances of sense and perception, there are some things that are grateful and others unwelcome to them, some things that they incline to, and others that they fly: but this makes nothing for innate characters on the mind, which are to be the principles of knowledge, regulating our practice. Such natural impressions on the understanding are so far from being confirmed hereby, that this is an argument against them, since, if there were certain characters imprinted by nature on the understanding, as the principles of knowledge, we could not but perceive them constantly operate in us and influence our knowledge, as we do those others on the will and appetite; which never cease to be the constant springs and motives of all our actions to which we perpetually feel them strongly impelling us.[15]

Locke further states that though all men necessarily pursue what they presume will make them happy, all men do not pursue the same things.

From what has been said it is easy to give an account how it comes to pass that, though all men desire happiness, yet their *wills carry them so contrarily*, and consequently some of them to what is evil. And to this I say that the various and contrary choices that men make in the world do not argue that they do not all pursue good, but that the same thing is not good to every man alike. . . .

The mind has a different relish, as well as the palate; and you will as fruitlessly endeavour to delight all men with riches or glory (which

15. Locke, Bk. 1 ch. 3, par. 3.

yet some men place their happiness in) as you would to satisfy all men's hunger with cheese or lobsters; which, though very agreeable and delicious fare to some, are to others extremely nauseous and offensive. And many people would with reason prefer the griping of an hungry belly to those dishes which are a feast to others. Hence it was, I think that the philosophers of old did in vain inquire whether *summum bonum* consisted in riches, or bodily delights, or virtue, or contemplation; and they might have as reasonably disputed, whether the best relish were to be found in apples, plums, or nuts, and have divided themselves into sects upon it. For, as pleasant tastes depend not on the things themselves but their agreeableness to this or that particular palate, wherein there is great variety, so the greatest happiness consists in the having those things which produce the greatest pleasure, and in the absence of those which cause any disturbance, any pain. Now these, to different men, are very different things.[16]

The skeleton of Pope's theory of the ruling passion is visible in these passages; certainly there is substantial agreement between Pope and Locke on many points in their attempts to describe men. The two men, nevertheless, are not carried in the same direction by their thought. Locke's passages might explain the presence of a ruling passion if he were to posit one, but that he does not do, and Pope's description of the world as mysteriously constructed by God so that agents will produce effects required by the system but of which they are unaware plays no role in Locke's psychological or political theory. The above passages from Locke do no more than explain the presence of different tastes; Pope's ruling passion is far more specific. Locke's observation that men pursue pleasure or happiness and avoid pain out of innate principle does not amount to positing a ruling passion in Pope's sense because in Pope's system all of those motivations are equally present, but the ruling passion is something different and additional.

A description of human motivation closer to Pope's and containing most of his distinctions can be found in Hobbes'

16. Ibid., Bk. 2, ch. 21, pars. 54–55.

Leviathan. Hobbes has been distinguishing between natural and acquired wit and has been describing the different varieties of both.

The causes of this difference of wits, are in the passions; and the difference of passions proceedeth, partly from the different constitution of the body, and partly from different education. For if the difference proceeded from the temper of the brain, and the organs of sense, either exterior or interior, there would be no less difference of men in their sight, hearing, or other senses, than in their fancies and discretions. It proceeds therefore from the passions; which are different, not only from the difference of men's complexions; but also from their difference of customs, and education.

The passions that most of all cause the difference of wit, are principally, the more or less desire of power, of riches, of knowledge, and of honour. All which may be reduced to the first, that is, desire of power. For riches, knowledge and honour, are but several sorts of power.

And therefore, a man who has no great passion for any of these things; but is, as men term it, indifferent; though he may be so far a good man, as to be free from giving offence; yet he cannot possibly have either a great fancy, or much judgment. For the thoughts are to the desires, as scouts, and spies, to range abroad, and find the way to the things desired: all steadiness of the mind's motion, and all quickness of the same, proceeding from thence: for as to have no desire, is to be dead: so to have weak passions, is dullness; and to have passions indifferently for every thing, GIDDINESS, and *distraction;* and to have stronger and more vehement passions for any thing, than is ordinarily seen in others, is that which men call MADNESS.[17]

This passage from *Leviathan* is more detailed than Pope's discussion of the ruling passion, and some of Hobbes' conclusions are different from Pope's, but the final description is nearly the same. Hobbes attributes the great passion to complexion (plus customs and education),[18] and he asserts that a

17. Hobbes, *Leviathan,* ch. 8.
18. Hobbes also mentions the passion a little later: "For the variety of behaviour in men that have drunk too much, is the same with that of madmen: some of them raging, others loving, others laughing, all extravagantly, but according to their several domineering passions . . ." (ibid.).

mastering passion concentrates a man's actions and gives him purpose and direction (that is, it prevents giddiness and distraction).[19] These are also basic elements in Pope's theory. For Pope the ruling passion derives from man's physical constitution (the organs determine his disposition for him), and the ruling passion serves the purpose of directing man to "a certain coast." Hobbes' limitation of the passions to desire for power, while not a part of Pope's system, is not contrary to its spirit, and Pope puts Hobbes' four passions at the top of his list:

> **Let pow'r or knowledge, gold or glory, please,**
> **Or (oft more strong than all) the love of ease. . . .**
>
> (II, 169–70)

Hobbes' notion that a predominant passion carried to an extreme is madness also comes within the spirit of Pope's warnings to keep the master passion under control.[20] Hobbes, may, on the other hand, be weighing the argument in Pope's more positive direction with the insinuating wording that strong passions are what "men call MADNESS."

These similarities need not put Pope overtly into the Hobbesian camp (if there was any such thing) on this or any subject. For although some of Hobbes' most characteristic ideas were

19. ". . . [God] ordained this great diversity of *Ingenies* among them [men], as a means to accommodate them to mutual assistance and association" (Walter Charleton, *Two Discourses* [London, 1669], pp. 39–40).

20. Pope's position is made particularly clear in the "Epistle to Bathurst," where he concludes that though great passions may be folly, being without any is greater folly still.

> "All this is madness," cries a sober sage:
> But who, my friend, has reason in his rage?
> "The ruling Passion, be it what it will,
> "The ruling Passion conquers Reason still."
> Less mad the wildest whimsey we can frame,
> Than ev'n that Passion, if it has no Aim;
> For tho' such motives Folly you may call,
> The Folly's greater to have none at all.
>
> (153–60)

In the lines which follow he quotes from the *Essay on Man* (II, 205–6) and says that God directs the passion to proper and constructive ends.

proving useful to conservative causes, as we have seen in Waterland's contention with Sykes, Hobbes' influence was not something that any writer would want to acknowledge. *Leviathan* as a text is sufficiently difficult so that three hundred years have not solved its problems or settled what Hobbes intended to say, but his contemporaries and immediate successors in psychological and political theorizing made small attempt to represent him accurately. They reacted to isolated ideas very strongly and usually negatively. But there is little else in Hobbes beside his relatively pessimistic assessment of man that would cause any sympathetic vibrations in Pope's poem.

There are also some slight differences between Pope's and Hobbes' thought on the ruling passion itself. Pope appears to mean that each man has a ruling passion; Hobbes limits so strong a motivation to a superior few. In addition, in Pope's system the presence of a ruling passion is finally mitigated by the intention of God, who arranges things in such a way that the system will always be served. Pope describes a ruling virtue grafted onto the ruling passion and makes it responsible for the strength of a man's drive to virtue. Mandeville and La Rochefoucauld intend only to demonstrate man's lack of virtue when they describe ruling passions such as pride and shame, and some such motivation applies to Hobbes as well. Pope's grafting of the ruling virtue onto the ruling passion bears some similarity to the intentions of more benevolent writers such as Butler and Shaftesbury, but his insistence that self-love is the final motivation in every act shows that he intends the reader to think of man as something other than a creature of natural, abstract benevolence.

Pope has, in fact, combined various ideas about a predominant passion into a system that transforms them into something quite different from what they are in other sources. He admits that the passion exists, though in some systems such an admission would damn both God and man; but he puts it to work in a universe where it fulfills a need and conduces to what, in that system, is virtue. We find him here on a ground quite separated from both the schools of benevolence and self-love, though he shares important ideas with each, and he quite wittily manipulates his ideas in a way contrary to what must have been contemporary expectation.[21]

If one is concerned with Pope's manipulation of ideas as well as verbal similarities, there is another controversy quite distant from the one already noticed that shows an equally interesting parallel. The controversy is theological rather than psychological, but it uses a similar argument to solve a similar difficulty. In order to see the parallel, one need only remember that, as Pope defends it, the ruling passion is useful to an observer of men for the purpose of seeing through the apparent aimlessness of human action to a unifying pattern. If one can but find out the ruling passion that possesses any man one will be able to observe that those actions which appear to be uncoordinated and at cross purposes are drawn into a coherent pattern. Both the man thus analyzed and his species are vindicated from the charge of being aimless and ill-conceived, because individual men are in fact quite understandable.

Chapter 2 of the present study shows how Pope vindicates God from a similar charge. The imaginary antagonist against whom Pope argues insisted that certain facts of the world are inconsistent with infinite goodness and that others are inconsistent with infinite justice. Our customary concept of God is apparently torn apart by these inconsistencies. To vindicate God from this charge, Pope shows the total creation to be consistent with the demands of the ruling attribute of reason to which every other consideration is subordinate. In following this path Pope makes use of an argument that was familiar to his contemporaries. John Balguy, a clergyman and disciple of Samuel Clarke, gives a particularly clear statement:

More particularly I would observe, in respect of God's *Moral Perfections*, how prone we seem to distinguish and multiply them beyond

21. As support for some of the above discussion (but not all) see Bertrand Goldgar, "Pope's Theory of the Passions: The Background of Epistle II of the *Essay on Man*," *Philological Quarterly* 41 (1962): 730–43.

measure, and, as I apprehend, without sufficient Grounds. Unmindful
of that *Simplicity* of the Divine Nature, which is itself an undoubted
Perfection; we frame to ourselves, instead of an uniform Principle
of Action, a great Variety of distinct Attributes. The Consequence of
which is, not only a Diminution of the great Idea, but an Introduction
of divers Difficulties and Perplexities of Conception which would
otherwise be avoided.

However we may divide and distinguish God's Moral Attributes,
according to the different Effects, Dealings and Dispensations
resulting from them; yet in themselves they seem to be but one and
the same Perfection variously exercised on different Objects and
Occasions, and in different Cases and Circumstances; and cannot
therefore, without Error and Inconvenience, be consider'd as distinct
Attributes. The Perfection I am speaking of, is that of God's determining himself by *Moral Fitness*, or acting perpetually according to
the *Truth, Nature*, and *Reasons of Things*. His Justice, Righteousness,
Truth, Faithfulness, Holiness, Goodness, Mercy, Longsuffering, and
whatever other moral Characters may be ascribed to him, do all
center in this Idea, and may properly be reduced to this single Principle. They are all comprehended in that *Moral Rectitude* or Righteousness, by which all the Divine Actions are unalterably conducted.
Whether God visit Men in Mercy or Judgment, with Blessings or
Calamities; whether he execute Sentence speedily, or suspend it for
a long Time; the same sacred Rule is equally, and constantly, and
inviolably observ'd by Him.[22]

Balguy is aware that scripture speaks of various moral characteristics, but he dismisses that verbal usage as "only by way of
Accommodation to human Language, and human Conception."[23]

Human observation is the source of the difficulty men have
in reconciling God's various attributes. People bewilder themselves attempting to find the boundaries of God's justice and
goodness, but they would not do so if they reflected that God
always does what is "right and reasonable, and fit." Actual

22. John Balguy, *Divine Rectitude: Or, a Brief Inquiry Concerning the
Moral Perfections of the Diety: Particularly in respect of Creation and
Providence* (London, 1730), pp. 4–5.
23. Ibid., p. 5.

mercy and goodness, then, would be what is in harmony with the predominant principle of rectitude. Balguy is arguing here on the side of Samuel Clarke for the reason of things as the foundation of action and morality, but that aspect of the argument may be referred to the Waterland-Sykes controversy described above.[24] Balguy is sensible that his argument for rectitude could be said to produce a mathematical and heartless world, but he denies this consequence. He asserts that though the motive for forming the world was the *"Production of Happiness,"* this purpose did not commit God to ignore other values.

And the more we examine His Works, the more Reason we shall find to conclude, that He would suffer nothing to come out of his Hands, which was not agreeable to *Order,* and perfect in its Kind. Not only every Individual is *fearfully and wonderfully made,* but a vast Variety of Species are fixed in a regular and beautiful Subordination; ascending from inanimate and stupid Matter to Human Kind, and reaching beyond it higher and further than our Faculties are able to follow them. Nay, it may reasonably be conjectured, that there are more Orders and Ranks of Beings above us, than beneath us; all contributing to make up that Scale, that System of Creatures, which no Wisdom less than infinite could contrive, no Power less than infinite accomplish.[25]

Balguy's principle of rectitude pushes him to exactly the same conclusion that Pope's choice of infinite wisdom led to: a principle of order superseding individual, isolated pieces of goodness. Balguy is free to say, with Pope, that God acts from moral necessity.[26] His conclusion regarding the relationship of man's happiness to the good of the whole is also familiar.

That as much *Happiness* was produced, and provided for, as was consistent with the *Order* and Perfection of the Universe, may perhaps be more properly supposed, than *vice versa.*[27]

24. See above, pp. 115–25.
25. Balguy, *Divine Rectitude,* pp. 13–14.
26. Ibid., p. 14.
27. Ibid.

All apparent evil in the system is doubtless real good, and if there are any real evils they are the product of creatures rather than God.[28]

Important to Balguy's scheme is his insistence that the qualities of things (beauty is a special example) are not relative to our perception of them. Nor are they a product of the accommodation of our senses to the objects we perceive to be lovely (as would be the result with Francis Hutcheson's sense of beauty), but qualities of excellence in the objects themselves. We perceive them intellectually to be what they are. God is committed to a single set of excellences because no relativity can intervene to take the rough edges off the absolute relationship upon which the qualities of all objects depend. Balguy's total purpose is a vindication of God from responsibility for the origin of evil, and his basic defense is God's predominant attribute of rectitude to which all partial concerns are finally subservient and in the face of which all partial ill becomes good.

Thomas Bayes, F. R. S., replied to Balguy in 1731 in *Divine Benevolence: Or, an Attempt to Prove the Principle End of the Divine Providence and Government is the Happiness of his Creatures*. Bayes provided a set of observations that make some important issues particularly clear. His text defends the moral attributes and attempts to keep them from being swallowed by the Aaron's serpent of divine rectitude, but it is not so much the principle of a predominant attribute that he objects to as the particular one that Balguy chose. His reasons are ingenious.

Now, as the desire of some end must be the motive to any action, so 'tis the nature of the end designed, and which the action is proper to effect that renders it good or bad, fit or unfit to be performed. When therefore we say, that God is in all his Actions governed by the reasons and fitness of things, we must, I think, mean, if we would understand ourselves, that he is moved to every action by a regard to some good and valuable end, and always chuses that way of

28. Ibid., p. 15.

conduct which is most proper to bring about the end designed. This seems to be the only notion we have of a wise and reasonable action, and *this end* ought to be taken notice of in the description of divine rectitude.

Thus, for instance, if you suppose with me, that the view by which the divine being is directed in all his actions, is a regard to the greatest good or happiness of the universe, then the moral rectitude of God may be thus described, *viz.* That it is a disposition in him to promote the general happiness of the universe. . . .[29]

Bayes is rejecting Balguy's retreat toward order by denying that order is a sufficient principle of operation. He insists that one would have to ask why order would be valued by divine rectitude, and he insists that the answer could not be, as Balguy says it is, that order is valuable for its own sake. Such questions are relative to an end beyond them.

The first thing therefore that we have to do before we can determine any thing concerning the moral perfections of God, or hope to solve the difficulties relating to the conduct of his providence, is to find out what it is that renders actions fit to be performed, or what is the end that a good and virtuous being, as such, is in pursuit of.[30]

Rectitude is no such principle, though benevolence, or the desire to produce the most good to creatures, is.[31] Bayes is, then, not objecting to giving God a ruling attribute in order to explain the phenomena of the world and explain away apparent conflicts. He is objecting to Balguy's choice of attributes. But here one must observe that by his appeal to a superior purpose and value Balguy intends to account for apparent evils which exist, while Bayes denies the existence of even apparent evils. The attempt we find in Pope and Balguy to show the necessity or unavoidability of friction by an appeal to the excellence of the whole machine must be distinguished from Bayes' insistence

29. Thomas Bayes, *Divine Benevolence: Or an Attempt to Prove that the Principle End of Divine Providence and Government is the Happiness of his Creatures* (London, 1731), p. 14.

30. Ibid., p. 15.

31. Ibid., p. 16.

that there is no friction. In fact Bayes' position is that partial evil is universal good.[32]

Bayes' discussion of these problems leads him to prefer self-love to the reason of things as a principle of morality because of the essential yardstick that only an act's tendency to produce pleasure or pain can determine whether it is good or bad. It is worth noting here that Bayes' distinction when applied to man is in harmony with Pope's, but when it is applied to God their positions diverge. There Pope is on Balguy's side. Pope's system leads to a dualism. There are two motives for action. One is the reason of things, and the other is one's reward for doing the action; the former motivates God, the latter man. This aspect of Bayes' interesting argument, however, is not important to the present problem. The important point is that he denies the predominance of rectitude and asserts the predominance of benevolence, and in doing so he shows that, from two points of view, observed inconsistencies in the system of the world can be resolved by an appeal to a predominant attribute to which all other motivation becomes subservient.

To summarize, to Pope's contemporaries, when various motives of supposedly unified beings appeared to conflict, one piece of dialectical weaponry that was available for denying the apparent conflict was an appeal to the existence of a higher or more inclusive characteristic into which lesser motives could be subsumed. The argument is largely an appeal for altered, heightened, broadened perspective, for looking at the various individual actions from the enlightened awareness that follows upon a knowledge of ultimate ends and goals. Using this argument to vindicate God from the apparent evils of the world was common enough, but Pope's use of the same argument to show that man, too, is a less chaotic creature than he seems was apparently less usual.

32. Ibid., pp. 32–33.

7

Self-love as the Motivation to Action

Most of the important points concerning Pope's handling of self-love as the predominant motivating force of human nature have been touched upon, but the idea is of sufficient importance to his system to warrant separate attention even though some repetition may result. Probably the best starting place is still Hobbes. As we have seen, Hobbes' ideas were frequently useful in orthodox argument even though his name was anathema. His assessment of man was not very glorious, but it made the need for established religion and unimpeachable authority in government plausible, and it stood, in one way or another, as an attack on the fountain source of human pride.

Of Hobbes' ideas pertinent to the present discussion, two are at the heart of what various controversial works cited as the issue in the assessment of man's ruling motivation. Hobbes was at least widely assumed to have asserted that all men are motivated entirely by self-love. From this observation he concluded that men are naturally at war with one another. If they are naturally at war with one another, then the disposition toward the good of one's fellow men, which is the defining criterion for virtue in many ethical works, plays no role in human nature.

This argument could be attacked both at the first assertion and at the conclusion stemming from it. Some writers deny that man is motivated exclusively by self-love. Others deny that the motivation by self-love is necessarily destructive to virtue, and a third argument of some importance questions the notion that man is guided in his actions involving his fellow men by "human nature." Upholders of this last argument assert that men are motivated in their moral actions by laws and commands they receive from God or government or some other power above individual human nature. To these writers human nature in the form of self-love or self-protection may compel men to obey the laws rather than suffer the consequences, but the actual source of the law itself is extrahuman. To these writers, human nature is something men must rise above.

One difficulty encountered by a twentieth-century student who wishes to establish the status of the idea that self-love is the dominant force in human nature is the ambiguity with which Pope's contemporaries used the term. The barest meaning of the words will obviously be quite stable; there is a positive feeling toward some concept of self. The way in which, to various writers, this positive feeling manifested itself, or the form it took, varied from context to context so that writers who assess self-love are not always referring to the same psychological impulse. The term sometimes meant selfishness,[1] some-

1. "Selfe-love then may bee defined, an inordinate inclination of the soule,

times self-preservation,[2] and sometimes love of the self as opposed to love of things outside of the self.[3]

The different attitudes toward self-love visible in the writings of the period are partly the result of these different definitions and partly a result of the use of a rigorous definition of virtue.[4] Pope integrates self-love harmlessly into his system by providing it with a meaning to some degree different from any of the three most frequent ones. He disarms the term by making it the principle of action in man; it is what causes men to move. It is the force, the opposite of lethargy, that prefers one thing to another, or prefers something to nothing. It must be present, and it must be stronger than the inactive and reflective principle because otherwise the creature would merely "draw nutrition, propagate, and rot." No strong psychological concept of self is necessary to this principle as Pope describes it, though

---

affecting too much the pleasures of the body against the prescript of right reason. . ." (Wright, p. 14). "*Self-love*. It is a vehement and inordinate inclination to ones own content in things carnall, earthly and sensual . . ." (the author then goes on to give three different kinds of self-love, two of which he can approve) (Edward Leigh, *A Systeme or Body of Divinity* [London, 1654], p. 379).

2. "Next to that natural *Self-love*, or Care of his own Preservation, which every one necessarily has in the first Place for *himself;* there is in all Men a certain natural Affection for their *Children and Posterity* . . ." (Samuel Clarke, *BLS,* 2:92). ". . . From this original Turn of Mind, whereby we are made susceptible of Pleasure and Pain, it naturally follows that we must necessarily delight in, and approve of our having pleasing Perceptions, and seek and pursue after them; but on the other Hand, hate Pain and avoid it: Which is what I understand in General, by Self-love, Self-preservation, or Self-interest" (Alexander Innes [Archibald Campbell], *An Enquiry into the Original of Moral Virtue* [Westminster, 1728], p. 193).

3. "Further, private happiness or good is all which self-love can make us desire, or be concerned about: in having this consists its gratification: it is an affection to ourselves; a regard to our own interest, happiness, and private good: and in the proportion a man hath this, he is interested, or a lover of himself. . . . On the other hand, particular affections tend towards particular external things: these are their objects; having these is their end . . ." (Butler, p. 140).

4. According to the rigoristic definition of virtue, it must have no tincture of self-love and, indeed, often must be contrary to self-love. I am following the terminology of F. B. Kaye in the introduction to his edition of Mandeville's *Fable of the Bees*. See especially pp. xlvii–xlviii.

self-love as selfishness lurks near at all times because that alone stirs the creature into action which it believes will bring it pleasure or pain. Benevolent interest in one's fellows is excluded at the outset as part of the natural motivation of such a creature, if benevolence must be totally unselfish. There is among Pope's contemporaries little or no argument that self-love to some degree exists. The issue that arises among the writers who agree that it exists as a powerful force comes from the extent to which it is supposed to triumph over more abstract concepts of virtue or benevolence or the extent to which it allows motivations for the good of other men, even if some tincture of self remains.

The substance of Pope's assertions about self-love is included in what he has to say about the passions, since the passions are the modes of self-love or the means through which self-love operates. Self-love, however, has an individual and single form as well as an embodiment in the passions, in much the same way that Pope thinks of reason as a total capacity as well as individual acts of reasoning. Each passion has as its object the pleasing of the self; therefore, the passions have a single focus or a point at which they converge. If observed from the opposite direction, all passions diverge from the single point of self-love. The receiver of the sensation is always the same, though each passion is different, and since that receiver is attracted to what brings it pleasure and repelled by what gives it pain, it is motivated by love for the self. This motivation toward good for the self does involve some danger, as Pope describes it, however, because, though its intention is always the same, self-love has no capacity for determining what acts or objects will fulfill its intention of personal happiness. Self-love is dependent on reason, for reason can accomplish the task of foreseeing actual consequences and avoiding mistakes that might arise from objects that do not actually have the capacity to please which they seem at a distance to possess.

In the context of Pope's own time, his assertions about self-love might easily become controversial when he grants that self-love is stronger than reason. His contemporaries frequently divided man into two principles, one speculative and inactive, the other impulsive and active. Though his giving the latter of the two principles the name *self-love* may be somewhat unusual, it is not much out of the common way; but to most writers the necessity for reason to dominate in this combination was fundamental, at least until orthodoxy found the way for predominant self-love to serve established religion by demonstrating the need for a revealed system of rewards and punishments. To Pope, however, predominant self-love is logically necessary. For the same reason that self-love must exist at all (to move the creature by means of the passions) it must be stronger than reason; reason would otherwise predominate and keep the creature in indolence, where it would "draw nutrition, propagate, and rot."

Two additional subsidiary conclusions on the existence of predominant self-love round out Pope's case. He says that self-love is intrinsically neither good nor evil but becomes one or the other by being properly or improperly followed, though he admits self-love to be dangerous because of its strength and lack of critical ability. Finally Pope equates self-love and social love in a way different from that of other writers who also equated them (for the equation itself was not unusual). For Pope, man, a necessarily self-loving creature, acts benevolently because the universe is so arranged that actions beneficial to his fellow men are necessary to fulfill his drive to self-love. The benevolence itself, if assessed according to the rigorous definition of virtue, would belong to God because it is he who created the universe so that man would find the good of other men to his advantage. Pope does not, therefore, make men benevolent in the sense that they love their fellow men without regard to personal reward. On the other hand, Pope seems to reject the rigorous definition of virtue as it applies to man, and he redefines the term so that what men do can count as virtue, because virtue comes to refer to the consequence rather than the intention of an action.

Predominant Self-Love

The present discussion can be limited to those writers who admitted that men were motivated *predominantly* by self-love. The range is wide. Malebranche admits the mastery of self-love.

> Nevertheless, the Inclination we should have for GOD is lost by the fall. But the inclination we ought to have for our own Preservation; or *our Self-love,* is so mightily increas'd, that 'tis at last become the absolute Master of our Will.[5]

But he does not regard the domination of self-love as either natural or defensible. It is a proof of man's sinful nature. A different reaction comes from John Clarke, the Hull schoolmaster. He argues that "there neither is, nor can be, any other Principle of human Conduct than Self-love, or a regard to Interest in this Life, or a future. . . ."[6] Clarke's purpose, however, is to prove that only future rewards and punishments can motivate men to virtue in this life. Jacques Esprit gives numerous examples to show that self-love dominates human action.

> But they [philosophers] had also perceiv'd at the same time, that since Self-love is become the Master and Tyrant of Man, it suffers in him no Virtue or good Action, but what is useful to it, and that it employs them all to compass its different aims and views. So that it is only with reference to the ends of Self-love, that Reason induces Men to have a respect for their Parents, to assist the Poor, and to observe the Laws of Justice. Thus they do not commonly perform all these Duties, but when they are acted by Self-love.[7]

Archibald Campbell, a professor in church history at St. Andrews, wrote to refute Mandeville, but he admits the supremacy of self-love from the outset.

> And to begin with that which is interwoven in the Constitution of all animate Beings: 'Tis very certain, that all Men have implanted in their Nature a Principle of Self-Love or Preservation, that irresistibly

5. Malebranche, *Search after Truth*, p. 147.

6. John Clarke (of Hull), p. 15.

7. Jacques Esprit, *Discourses on the Deceitfulness of Humane Virtues,* trans. William Beauvoir (London, 1706), sig. A5v.

operates upon us in all Instances whatsoever, and is the great Cause, or the first Spring of all our several Motions and Actions, which Way soever they may happen to be directed.[8]

To Campbell self-love is the foundation and base of virtue rather than its enemy. Part of man's self-love takes the direction of wanting company and wanting others to love him; out of self-love men do what other men would approve in order to gain their love. Campbell quarrels with Mandeville's insistence that acts done out of self-love are not virtuous, and he also insists that virtue is not relative or arbitrary but the product of the nature of things, of which the interplay of self-love with self-love is an essential part.[9]

Campbell represents almost completely Pope's position in the philosophical spectrum. Campbell refutes both Mandeville and Hutcheson, taking each of Hutcheson's examples of disinterestedness and proving it to be basically self-love, and yet he maintains the existence of virtuous action. Pope works in almost precisely the same way. One part of his assertions puts him on the side of Mandeville, La Rochefoucauld, and Espirit in reducing all of men's actions to self-love, but the conclusion they drew from this view, that there is no virtue, is not Pope's conclusion. On the other hand, Pope does not describe, with the other side of the controversy, any benevolent affections in men from which virtuous actions could stem (because he does not say that men are directed to the good of something other than the self). He does describe a conscience horrified by vice, and an ability to distinguish between vice and virtue as clearly as between black and white, but that ability does not serve any

8. Campbell, pp. 3–4.
9. Cf. the following: "And this Affection or Quality of any Action which we call *Merit* is very consistent with a Man's acting *ultimately* for his own private Happiness. For any particular Action that is undertaken *for the sake of another,* is *meritorious,* i.e., deserves Esteem, Favour, and Approbation from him for whose sake it was undertaken, towards the Doer of it" (John Gay, "Preliminary Dissertation," in King's *Origin of Evil,* p. xxv). This John Gay is not the author of the *Beggar's Opera.* He was a fellow of Sidney Sussex College, Cambridge, and later a vicar in Bedfordshire.

apparent function except the more efficient fulfillment of self-love. Pope's emphasis indicates that in any conflict between self-love and another principle, self-love would be the winner ("Vice or Virtue, self directs it still").

In order to understand Pope's final disposition of the idea that self-love is the dominating influence in all human activity, one must notice the notion which dominates every aspect of the *Essay*—that God disposes everything in such a way that the harmonious functioning of the whole creation is supported by the motivation of every creature. Here Pope's position is that men do all out of self-love, but self-love is so bound up with benevolence that self-love and social love are the same; in doing good for themselves men do good for their fellow men. Virtue, for Pope, is (as the line "Vice or Virtue, self directs it still" shows) the result of the outcome of an action rather than the intention behind it. Pope's position is, to be sure, not perfectly unequivocal, but a definition of virtue as an action directed toward the good of another (even though motivated originally by self-love) is the most congruent with his combination of weak reason and strong self-love.

A problem of interpretation arises with lines 93–100 of Epistle II. These lines have been interpreted in such a way as to attribute to Pope an espousal of the rigoristic definition of virtue, or something close to it. They are, however, capable of another interpretation, one that allows virtue to be based on self-love.

> Modes of Self-love the Passions we may call;
> 'Tis real good, or seeming, moves them all;
> But since not every good we can divide,
> And Reason bids us for our own provide;
> Passions, tho' selfish, if their means be fair,
> List under Reason, and deserve her care;
> Those, that imparted, court a nobler aim,
> Exalt their kind, and take some Virtue's name.
>   (II, 93–100)

In the lines preceding the final couplet, reason bids us provide for our own good when we cannot separate it from the good of our fellow men. Since reason does this, passions, so long as they use fair means, enlist under reason (presumably so that it will show them the way to fulfillment), "and deserve her care. . . ." But does the final couplet mean what Mack quotes Pattison as saying it means: "the passions when reason is imparted to them," "court a nobler aim,/Exalt their kind, and take some Virtue's name"? Is Pope saying that when reason is imparted to the passions they will court a nobler aim and be turned to virtues? Is reason the cause of virtue?

As the punctuation now stands, this interpretation seems most likely. As Mack's bibliographical notes show, however, the punctuation here, as in the Elwin-Courthope edition and others, is not Pope's but Warburton's. Mack lists three different ways in which Pope punctuated the line (but even then does not exhaust the variations), none of which is the same as Warburton's: "Those that *imparted,* . . ."; "Those that imparted, . . ."; "Those that, imparted, . . ." In two out of the three, the word *imparted* is given as heavy stress as punctuation can well afford, but in Warburton's punctuation (with *that* transformed into a demonstrative pronoun) the *that* would be stressed, altering the sense, or at very least the emphasis of the assertion. Warburton's reasons for wanting to punctuate the line in his way are sufficiently apparent so that one need not ponder over what could have moved him to it. If Pope stressed not *that* but *imparted,* the lines could mean that those passions which (*when* they are imparted to an object) court a nobler aim are what we call virtue. In other words, the couplet may suggest a functional, rather than intentional or rigoristic, definition of virtue. Pope, then, against Mandeville and others, would be saying that virtue is (merely?) a passion whose fulfillment results in social good; the intention of God, not the intention of man, is the force from which virtue stems. Certain other key lines strongly suggest such a definition.

> The surest Virtues thus from Passions shoot,
> Wild Nature's vigor working at the root.
>   (II, 183–84)

On the other hand, one need not make too much of this couplet because even with Warburton's punctuation the line could be saying only that in a system where self-love and social love are the same, reason will, if it is to perform its job in satisfying self-love, always see that they are the same and will lead men to virtue by leading them to true self-love. Whether or not Pope is denying the rigoristic definition of virtue in this couplet, he is certainly ready to do so at other times; even here his trust in reason for the job of finding virtue is contingent on the recognition that reason will provide "for our own."

Even in Pope's final disposition of the problem of the domination of self-love there is a similarity to the way in which Campbell treads between Mandeville and Hutcheson. Campbell too knits the world together so that each man's self-love enforces that of others and brings about a system of benevolence that glorifies God.

This is an Unlimited, universal Passion, whereby all Men are actuated, and without the Gratifying of which no Man can ever find himself easy among those Beings to whom he is associated. And as the *Desire* of *Esteem* Universally determines us to pursue *Love* towards Others, or to exert ourselves into all Virtuous Actions whatsoever (for these are the only Means, that can effectually recommend us to the *Good-Opinion* and *Love* of others) so from hence we cannot but have the most Elevated Apprehenshions of the Wonderful Goodness, and Wise Contrivance of the Great *Parent* of Mankind, who in the Nature of things, has determin'd us to pursue *Virtue*, with a View to raise such Affections (*Love* and *Esteem*) in other *Rational Agents,* as render them likewise Virtuous, or Morally Good towards us: By which Means, there is made the Best, and the amplest Provision possible, to secure every One's Ease and Comfort; We are all deeply engag'd in a Generous Contention, a Noble Plot, to promote each others Felicity; And if we follow this Divine Constitution of Things, we shall all endeavour, to the Utmost of our Power, to be

Joyful and Happy in One another through the whole Compass of our Duration.[10]

Pope's assertion that no one rests self-satisfied and that we are by God tricked into benevolence is certainly close to this final disposition of the problem in Campbell's system. In Pope's view, though, there is little or none of Campbell's sanguine assurance of man's virtue. This difference in the final color of their systems can largely be attributed to the emotional implications of what they variously assert. Pope's intention, like Mandeville's, is to mortify pride; man, as Pope sees him, is much the same as the creature described by Mandeville (or Hobbes), the same self-loving animal, capable of redemption only through the machinations of a benevolent creator or, in the case of Mandeville and Hobbes, of a prudent governor. Campbell's intention is more often supportive and perhaps inspirational so that he and Pope often differ on their perception of the consequences of what they say even though their assertions are similar.

Self-Love as a Neutral Force

While the reputation of self-love was never, at least in Christendom, very high, the earlier general attacks on it brought about a necessity to defend it, for its universality in all men's hearts, even if it was not thought the sole motivation of those hearts, was widely recognized. Many writers of Pope's time were disposed to justify self-love; and since no one would deny that self-love could exist in a destructive degree, an important observation was that it could be good as well. These writers wished to insist that not the motivation itself but its abuse held the danger.[11]

10. Campbell, pp. 332–33.
11. The following quotations all support the idea that it is not concern for the self which is bad but rather false or too vehement concern for the self. The effect of such an assertion is that self-love is good or bad depending on its degree or use. The same point is made in defending the passions in some cases.
"Self-love

The frequent attempts to vindicate self-love by separating
it from its abuse do not finally cast much light on Pope's own
vindication because usually the term is clearly not being used
in Pope's sense. Pope's concept of a single force feeding on
everything is really not amenable to an innocent or positive
assessment of the type that various writers applied to self-love
when they were thinking of it as self-preservation or at least as
a motivation capable of subservience to reason. As Pope defines
self-love it has already gone to the extreme which was unacceptable to most of its apologists. Except insofar as the term
self-love calls up so general a concept as that of being disposed
well to one's own needs, Pope's idea uses familiar words in a
less than familiar way. Other writers could vindicate self-love
by the assurance that it was weaker than reason and subject to

---

It is a vehement and inordinate inclination to ones own content in things
carnall, earthly, and sensual. . . .
    There is I. a natural . . . self-love, by which every one from the instinct of
nature loves himself, his own body, soul, life, *Eph.* 5.29, the Scripture doth
not condemn this.
    2. A divine self-love by which every one that is born again by the holy
Ghost from the instinct of the Spirit, loves himself, as is fitting, to the glory
of God and good of the Church. These two kindes of self-love were in
Christ.
    3. A devilish self-love, whereby one by the instinct of corrupt nature and
inflamed by Satan, so loves himself that he loves no other truly, and seeks
only his own things" (Leigh, p. 379).
    "If Almighty God would not have suffered Men to love themselves, he
would not have moved them to their Duty by their personal Benefit, and
especially by so great a Recompence as is that of Life Eternal.
    It would conduce to the Felicity of Men, even in this World, if they truly
loved themselves . . ." (Thomas Tenison, *A Sermon Against Self-Love, &c.
Preached before the Honourable House of Commons, on the 5th of June,
1689* [London, 1689], p. 5).
    "The highest and truest Self-love, is to love that which can alone make us
happy" (Wilkins, p. 209) (He is approvingly quoting Augustine). "For all our
Actions are design'd by us to some good which may arise to us; but we do
not always distinguish rightly of that good: we often mistake the *Bonum
apparens* for the *Bonum reale*" (Charles Blount, *The Oracles of Reason*
[London, 1693], p. 205 [article signed A.W.]). ". . . When self-love becomes
the *occasion* of *evil,* it is not by our following nature, but by perverting it"
(Chubb, p. 267).

rational control, but Pope vindicates it by showing that God makes use of it for purposes of which the creature may not be aware.

One vindication of the term that might profitably be compared with Pope's is to be found in Joseph Butler's sermons at the Rolls Chapel. Butler redeems self-love by redefining it according to philosophical principles, and he posits an assessment of man far more optimistic than Pope's. Butler is explicitly refuting the ideas of Hobbes and La Rochefoucauld "and this whole set of writers,"[12] and Pope's assertions concerning the predominance of self-love are similar to theirs, though his conclusions may differ. Butler admits that "no one can act but from a desire, or choice, or preference of his own,"[13] and he presents a distinction that he believes will describe human experience more accurately.

He maintains that there is a difference between loving the self and loving other objects, even though in all examples of loving, a relationship to the self may be fundamental. Only "cool or settled selfishness" should be called self-love, and "passive or sensual selfishness" should be distinguished from it. This cool selfishness wishes to bring happiness to the self, and anything that does not bring happiness to the self is out of harmony with its intention. Yet men do act where they know they will reap pain rather than pleasure. This is because various passions and appetites seek the enjoyment of objects that are adapted to them, but "it is not because we love ourselves that we find delight in such and such objects, but because we have particular affections towards them." But, he admits, "Take away these affections, and you leave self-love absolutely nothing at all to employ itself about."[14]

This latter qualification might be taken as an admission of Pope's point that "Modes of self-love the passions we may call," and a consequent admission that everything is done at bottom

12. Butler, *Works*, 1:16.
13. Ibid., p. 17.
14. Ibid., p. 18.

out of self-love; Butler denies this consequence, however, and insists that to love the self is to strive for its good, and to have passions and affections for other objects is to strive for those objects without regard to anything but experiencing them. He concludes that self-love is not too strong,[15] for every passion can outweigh it; most trouble and pain result from men's ignoring true, cool selfishness or sacrificing it in order to gratify a strong momentary passion.

Pope and Butler agree, then, that true self-love can be good if a man distinguishes between it and attractive things that will prove to be harmful if they are procured. Butler's distinction may be more semantically satisfactory, but, if so, it is because he is starting from quite a different set of assumptions. He intends to prove that benevolence, or a passion for the good of others, or disinterestedness, is not in conflict with self-love because it is one of the passions and is, therefore, satisfied with the attainment of its object. Pope's view of self-love denies the existence of passions and affections which have final objects other than pleasure for the self, and he is there in agreement with the group of writers of whom Butler specifically disapproves; yet both Pope and Butler defend self-love, and those writers of the school of selfishness do not. All that can be said is that Pope and Butler aim toward the same end but take quite divergent paths.

One must remember that the question at issue is not a semantic one; it is not a matter of what should or should not be *called* self-love. The issue is whether or not men have motivations toward the benefit of others that are beyond an expectation of personal reward. Butler's answer is that they do, and Pope's is that they do not. Butler's "cool or settled selfishness" seems to take for granted that what is good for the self can be determined and distinguished from what is bad for it. If the difference between good and bad were clear, then (in Butler's system) what is real self-love would be clear as well. It is true that reason can do much the same thing in Pope's system when

15. Ibid., p. 19.

reason is applied to a problem, but Pope's explanation of why men do things that prove hurtful would be that a mistake is made. Men hurt themselves not because they have affections for objects regardless of the effect on the self but because they make mistakes and do not realize what will cause harm. Pope's assessment of man is consequently quite different from Butler's and, one must remember, Pope's view is intended to make man think less well of himself and better of God.

Self-love and Social Love the Same

The idea that self-love is dangerous does not need separate attention, since the view is implicit in most of what has already been cited. The assertion that self-love and social love are the same represents a more important use of ideas. The idea itself is not particularly complex. It merely states that there is no conflict between actions done for the good of the self and those done for the good of society (or perhaps even the system) of which the creature is a part. At its simplest the idea is based on the observation that all beings are a part of something larger than themselves, that the creature is dependent on its surroundings for its own welfare. The creature will find that in order to exist as it desires it will derive benefit from doing what it can to help other parts of the system. If the proposition is stated negatively its effect is somewhat altered: socially beneficial actions are not antagonistic to the predominant principle of self-love because each man's good is bound up with the good of his fellow creatures.

The third epistle of the *Essay* gives Pope's case for the interaction of self-love and social love. He begins the epistle by describing the world as a "chain of love," with the creatures dependent on one another. He shows how all creatures benefit man and how man is beneficial to them as well. Here Pope comes close to asserting a natural benevolence in man, and such an interpretation is satisfactory if benevolence is defined in terms of results rather than intention; but the motivation Pope describes is not selfless:

> For some his Int'rest prompts him to provide,
> For more his pleasure, yet for more his pride:
> All feed on one vain Patron, and enjoy
> Th' extensive blessing of his luxury.
>
> (III, 59–62)

This vindication of relative weaknesses in creatures is also a vindication of God for having created weak creatures. One of the principles of coherence in the system of the universe is the weaknesses of the creatures that draw them together. Self-love and social love become the same because the universe is so arranged that weak creatures are dependent upon one another.

> God, in the nature of each being, founds
> Its proper bliss, and sets its proper bounds:
> But as he fram'd a Whole, the Whole to bless,
> On mutual Wants built mutual Happiness:
> So from the first eternal ORDER ran,
> And creature link'd to creature, man to man.
>
> (III, 109–14)

After giving a history of society that shows it is based on self-love extended by men as "they love themselves, a third time, in their race," and after asserting that government stems from love, Pope dwells on corruption and superstition and ties the whole system together by again asserting self-love to be the primary activating force.

> So drives Self-love, thro' just and thro' unjust,
> To one Man's pow'r, ambition, lucre, lust:
> The same Self-love, in all, becomes the cause
> Of what restrains him, Government and Laws.
> For, what one likes if others like as well,
> What serves one will, when many wills rebel?
> How shall he keep, what, sleeping or awake,
> A weaker may surprise, a stronger take?
> His safety must his liberty restrain:
> All join to guard what each desires to gain.
> Forc'd into virtue thus by Self-defence,
> Ev'n Kings learn'd justice and benevolence:

> Self-love forsook the path it first pursu'd,
> And found the private in the public good.
>
> (III, 269–82)

He ends the epistle with an enthusiastic approval of the soul's motion as it regards the whole; the position has special qualities because of the way in which social love is motivated.

> Man, like the gen'rous vine, supported lives;
> The strength he gains is from th' embrace he gives.
> On their own Axis as the Planets run,
> Yet make at once their circle round the Sun:
> So two consistent motions act the Soul;
> And one regards Itself, and one the Whole.
> Thus God and Nature link'd the gen'ral frame,
> And bade Self-love and Social be the same.
>
> (III, 311–18)

The fourth epistle adds to the complex concept that self-love and social love are the same the notion that all men are motivated toward happiness and the assurance that true happiness rests in the fulfillment and promotion of the common good (IV, 35–46). Pope stresses again and again that the benevolent tendency is a result of God's plan and comes from self-love; so he remains divorced from Shaftesburian benevolence and good will.

> Self-love thus push'd to social, to divine,
> Gives thee to make thy neighbour's blessing thine.
> . . . .
> Self-love but serves the virtuous mind to wake,
> As the small pebble stirs the peaceful lake. . . .
>
> (IV, 353–54, 363–64)

Mack says that asserting self-love and social love to be the same was "the central theme of much ethical writing in Pope's time and before."[16] In relation to this point special attention should be given to the views of Butler, Samuel Clarke, and Shaftesbury.[17] In all three such an assertion is part of a system-

16. Mack, p. 126n.
17. Mack quotes as follows: "The Endeavour, to the utmost of our power,

atic defense of benevolence, and the system of each is opposed
in important respects to that of Pope. Clarke counsels a reasonable imitation of the attributes of God. Shaftesbury and Butler
assert in varying degrees that men possess natural affections
toward social good and natural delight in the accomplishment
of socially beneficial actions. All three represent man in a more
conventionally positive light than Pope does. Archibald Campbell is nearer to Pope, though their assessments of man are at

---

of promoting the common Good of the whole System of rational Agents,
conduces . . . to the Good of every Part, in which our own Happiness, as
that of a Part, is contain'd" (Richard Cumberland, *A Treatise of the Laws
of Nature*, p. 16). "These ends do indeed perfectly coincide; and to aim at
public and private good are so far from being inconsistent, that they
mutually promote each other . . ." (Butler, p. 27). See also: "For since God
has plainly so constituted the nature of Man, that they stand continually in
need of each other's Help and Assistance, and can never live comfortably
without Society and mutual Friendship; and are indued with the faculties of
Reason and Speech, and with other natural Powers, evidently fitted to enable them to assist each other, in all matters of Life, and mutually to promote universal Love and Happiness; it is manifestly agreeable to Nature,
and to the *Will of God* who gave them these Faculties, that they should employ them wholly to this regular and good End" (Samuel Clarke, *BLS 2:109*).
"That to be well affected towards the publick interest and one's own, is not
only consistent, but inseparable: and that moral rectitude, or virtue, must
accordingly be the advantage, and vice the injury and disadvantage of every
creature" (Shaftesbury, 1:282). "For as it is Impossible, that *Self-Interest*,
can ever be Inconsistent with *Virtue*, but only the Deceitful Shadow of it,
which I own, is grasped at by every deluded Imagination, to his own Ruin,
and the great Disturbance of the World; So every Wise Man who follows
Nature, takes up *Virtue* and Utility under the same *Ideas*, determines them
by the same Rule, and he knows that these are only two Words that signify
the same Thing (as plainly appears from what I have hitherto said) which
he steadily pursues to the Unspeakable Pleasure and Happiness of himself,
and a whole System of *Rational Agents*" (Campbell, pp. 308–9). "And I may
add, that the better to cause Men to observe those Rules, which make for
their mutual Benefit, infinite Goodness has sown in their Hearts Seeds of
Pity, Humanity and Tenderness, which, without much difficulty, cannot be
eradicated; but nothing operates more strongly than that Desire Men have
of being in Esteem, Credit, and Reputation with their Fellow Creatures; not
to be obtain'd without acting on the Principles of natural Justice, Equity,
Benevolence, *etc*." (Matthew Tindal, *Christianity as Old as the Creation*
[London, 1730], p. 16).

least slightly different since Campbell puts such heavy stress on man's desire to be loved by his fellow men.

In his attitudes toward self-love Pope shows, as he has in other areas, a disposition to combine and adapt ideas in order to produce a system between contemporary extremes. He adopts the widely known attitude of Hobbes, Mandeville, Esprit, and La Rochefoucauld by admitting that all human actions are the product of self-love. To that attitude, however, he adds a definition of virtue that allows man to be self-loving and virtuous at the same time. Consequently, he denies these authors' conclusions that there is no virtue in men because there is no selflessness in them. He then posits a benevolent system (a concept irrelevant to the school of selfishness but cherished by the benevolists), but the benevolence of the system stems from God's structuring of the creation rather than the altruism of the creatures.

Thus Pope uses the ideas that were applied to the questions at hand by two opposing factions in an important philosophical argument and manages to produce a position between the extremes by adapting and modifying and adjusting the ideas so that they come to have a substantially different force, even meaning, in a system that it is at once largely familiar and wittily unconventional.

Conclusion

The foregoing chapters are not particularly thesis-laden; therefore, there is not much need to fire off a final volley of support for an unfamiliar position. It is true that I have suggested several times that I believe Pope's "steering betwixt extremes ... seemingly opposite" may have taken the form of adapting ideas while altering either the assumptions upon which they were based or the consequences which were supposed to result from them. However, this volume would be a ponderous piece of machinery with which to explicate this single sentence from Pope's prefatory statement regarding his "design." My main intention has been, I hope, somewhat more substantial. What I have wanted to do is describe the intellectual climate relevant to some of Pope's important ideas; if the description is not misleading, I have accomplished my aim.

I have also reached some conclusions which I might share with the reader, though I do not believe their acceptance to be crucial to my purpose. The most important has to do with Pope. I did not start out to vindicate him against charges of incompetence or not knowing the meanings of his own ideas, but to my mind I have done so anyway. Pope seems to be back on solid ground today after some very slippery going during much of the nineteenth century; so I do not anticipate having to argue very hard to gain the concession that his thinking was not as watery as some of his earlier readers believed. This does not commit either me or the reader to the position that Pope was one of the world's great philosophical minds, but it does not appear to me that we have any reason to rate him very low on the scale of understanding what he was saying as his own immediate readers might have understood it.

Of course Pope's material is rather difficult in this regard. The sort of thing we have in the *Essay on Man* virtually begs to be evaluated on grounds of its being right or wrong. If one agrees with the ideas in the poem, Pope will very likely seem to be a profound thinker, but if a reader is of a different mind, Pope will have misunderstood even the rudiments of what he was saying. Pope has been cursed in this manner with the Whitwell Elwins of the world who have no doubt that they know the truth in every argument. The abstract truth of what Pope is saying is not the only perception worthy of notice in his work. The fun in the *Essay on Man* is with Pope's performance, not with the validity of the philosophy. It is with watching an agile mind at work playing with ideas as with the pieces on a chess board, and I must say that as I have come to see Pope's mind at work it is at least the mind of an architect rather than a milliner. The notion that Pope merely dressed and decorated ideas that he neither understood nor appreciated seems, in the contemporary context that I have outlined, quite untenable.

Back in the dark past when I began reading with the purpose of understanding Pope's accomplishment more fully, I intended to cover all the ideas in the *Essay on Man*. I do not recall that I held that preposterous aim for more than two weeks, but it has certainly long been out of my expectations. I hope that I will not be taken in what I have done to have generalized about all of Pope's ideas. It may well be that some of his ideas in the *Essay* bear an entirely different relationship to their context, but I am prepared neither to affirm nor deny this possibility.

To my mind, the basic humanistic endeavor is to make all

of history contemporary, and if this volume has cast any light at all on the conceptual vocabulary and intellectual sensitivities of the first third of the eighteenth century, my labors will have been rewarded. If it has made Pope's mind any more accessible to his twentieth-century readers, the reward will be substantially increased, for it is Pope who matters most of all.

Index

Affections, natural, 110
Alphonsus X, of Spain, 15
Analogy, reasoning by, 48, 77–81
Ancients and moderns, 159n
Anderson, Ruth Leila, 155n
Arianism, 118
Aristotle, 45, 47
Asper, character in Jonson's *Every Man Out*, 155–57
Atheists, 14, 95
Audra, E., 107n
Augustine, St., 46, 52, 184n
Authority, need for in government and religion, 12, 115, 124, 173, 183
Ayloffe, William, 135n

Bacon, Francis, 88, 161
Baglivi, George, 160n
Balguy, John, 167–72; quoted, 167–69
Ball, John, 135n, 136n
Baptism, 117
Barrow, Isaac, quoted, 47
Bayes, Thomas, 170–72; quoted, 170–71

Bayle, Pierre, 13, 161n
Beauty, sense of, 170
Beddevole, Dominique, 159n
Benevolence: divine, 170–71; human, 129, 130, 166, 176, 186, 187, 189–91; school of, 166–67, 191; of creation, 127, 136, 191
Bible, analogical vocabulary of, 81
Blancard, Stephen, 159n
Blount, Charles, 184n
Blount, Sir Thomas Pope, quoted, 88n
Boas, George, 108n
Bolingbroke, Henry St. John, 1st Viscount, 14, 16, 39n; quoted, 14, 40n
Bond, Donald F., 141n
Boyce, Benjamin, 160n
Boyle, Robert, 11, 49, 50, 73, 108n
Boyle lectures, 11, 25n, 78
Bragge, Francis, 135n
Brauer, Robert Van Akin, 151n
Browne, Peter, 79–81, 83, 92, 92n, 94, 104; quoted, 80, 81, 83, 84n, 92, 93, 94
Bulwer, John, 133n, 134n; quoted, 133n

Burghope, George, 135n
Burnett, Thomas, 78, 81n; quoted, 78
Burthogge, Richard, 46, 50–56, 72; quoted, 50, 51, 52, 53, 54
Butler, Joseph, 31–32, 104, 105, 110, 113, 128–32, 166, 185–87, 189; quoted, 32, 129, 130, 131, 132, 175n, 185, 190n

Cambridge Platonists, 70
Campbell, Archibald, 178–79, 182–83, 190–91; quoted, 175n, 178–79, 182–83, 190n
Caryll, John, Sr., 43, 45
Causes, second, 53
Certainty, mathematical, in moral propositions, 21, 121n
Chain of being, 19, 33–35, 41, 43–44, 77, 152, 169
Chambers, Ephraim, 157n
Chambre. See Cureau de la Chambre, Marin
Charleton, Walter, 135n, 165n
Cheyne, George, 77
Choice, arbitrary. See Will, arbitrary
Christianity: necessity of, 11, 11n, 121; reasonableness of, 12
Chubb, Thomas, 116, 134, 136, 184
Clarke, John, 64–70, 66n, 116; quoted, 65, 66–67
Clarke, John, of Hull, 66, 66n, 101–103, 119–20, 121, 122, 135; quoted, 178
Clarke, Samuel, 27–29, 64, 115, 121, 167, 169, 189; quoted, 28, 83n, 86n, 175n, 190n
Common sense, 90
Comparing power, reason as, 97
Compass, reason as, 97, 141, 141n
Congreve, William, 157n
Conscience, 104, 137, 179
Conybeare, John, quoted, 84n
Craig, Hardin, quoted, 155n
Crane, Ronald S., 11n, 138n; quoted, 11n

Creation: arbitrariness of, 64, 70; special, 17–18, 59, 74, 98
Cudworth, Ralph, 21, 25, 39, 46, 70, 72, 113; quoted, 21, 25
Culverwell, Nathanael, 112–14; quoted, 112, 113–14
Cumberland, Richard, quoted, 190n
Cureau de la Chambre, Marin, 135n

Deism, 11, 105, 118, 121; defined, 11n; natural religion and, 11n, 12
Deists, 12n, 14, 15, 16n, 78, 95
Delany, Patrick, 40n
Descartes, René, 20–24, 26; quoted, 22, 23, 24
Determinism, psychological, 158
Differences of things. See Things, differences of
Dispensations, unequal, proof of immortality, 14–16
Ditton, Humphry, 135n
Dryden, John, 85n, 160, 160n; quoted, 157n, 160n
Duties, moral and positive, 116–20

Elwin-Courthope edition of Pope's works, 181; quoted, 141n
Emlyn, T., 116
Equilibrium, of humors, virtue in, 152–54
Esprit, Jacques, 10, 178, 179, 191
Eucharist, 117
Evil: as defect or imperfection, 17, 57–59, 66, 68; moral, 17–18, 54, 58, 60–63, 65, 66–70; natural, 17, 58, 59; origin of, 7, 10, 14, 44–45, 50, 56–70, 170; partial, as universal good, 14, 71, 170, 172; physical, 54

Faith, implicit, 124
Fall of man, 137
Fatalism, 29–30
Fitzgerald, Mary Margaret, 109n

Franklin, Benjamin, quoted, 101
Free will, 60–64; divine, 7, 10, 13, 20–30, 36, 122; human, 22, 158
Fulness, necessary, 59, 75

Gally, Henry, 160n
Gataker, Thomas, 52
Gay, John, 179n
Glover, Phillips, 116n
God: incomprehensibility of, 81, 85; moral attributes of, 25n, 39n, 170; predominant attribute of, 30–33, 167–72; self-existence of, 58; vindication of, 127, 167, 170, 188. See also Soul of the world
Goldgar, Bertrand, 167n
Good, universal, 71
Goodness, as God's predominant attribute, 31–33, 60
Grace, 136
Gulliver's Travels, 138n

Hakewill, George, 48n
Happiness, as final aim of creation, 9, 130, 169
Harris, John, 85n
Harvey, Gideon, 160n
Harvey, William, 159
Hazard, Paul, 109n
Herbert, Edward, 1st Baron Herbert of Cherbury, 16n, 105; quoted, 105
Hobbes, Thomas, 75, 105, 115, 119, 124, 136, 163–66, 173–74, 183, 185, 191; quoted, 133n, 164, 164n
Hooker, Edward N., 160
Hope, 109
Humors: all bodily fluids, 159; the four, 150, 159; necessary balance of, 150, 153; psychology of, 150–60; rejection of ancient theories of, 159–60, 159n; uncontrollability of, 155–57
Humors characters, 151–60, 157–58n

Hutcheson, Francis, 170, 179, 182

Ideas, innate, 162
Imagination, 87
Immensity, God's attribute of, 44, 46, 48
Innate capacities or principles, 109, 162
Innes, Alexander. See Campbell, Archibald
Instinct, 98–99

James, Robert, 160n
Jenyns, Soame, 152
Johnson, Samuel, 152
Johnson, Thomas, 116n
Jonson, Ben, 151, 153–59, 161; Every Man Out of His Humour. quoted, 154–55, 156
Justification, by faith or works, 117

Kaye, F. B., 175n
King, Archbishop William, 11, 28n, 31, 33, 34–39, 56–64, 65–70, 78, 134, 179n; quoted, 33, 34–35, 36, 37–38, 57, 58, 59, 61, 63, 64, 134

La Rochefoucauld, François, 10, 10n, 75, 105, 124, 166, 179, 185, 191
Law, Edmund, 25n, 31, 57, 57n; quoted, 25n, 31, 85n
Laws, general, 49, 68
Le Grand, Antoine, 127; quoted, 127–28
Leibniz, Gottfried Wilhelm von, 20–21, 22, 27–31, 33, 39, 39n, 64, 70, 122; quoted, 27, 29, 30
Leigh, Edward, 175n, 183–84n
Lemnius, Levinus, 155n
Liberty. See Free will
Locke, John, 86, 92, 94, 104, 104n, 161–63; quoted, 162–63

Lovejoy, Arthur O., 20, 34, 108n
Lucretius, 13

Mack, Maynard, 104, 181, 189, 189n
Mackworth, Sir Humphry, 48n
MacLean, Kenneth, 161
Malebranche, Nicholas, 48n, 82–83, 83n, 89, 92–94, 104n, 105, 178; quoted, 82, 89, 92, 93, 178
Mandeville, Bernard, 75, 102, 105, 124, 135n, 136, 161n, 166, 175n, 179, 181, 182, 191
Manichean heresy, 13
Manley, Mrs. Mary De La Riviere, 160n
Marcus Aurelius, 52, 127
Master passion. See Passion, predominant or ruling
Mechanism, world as a, 45, 49
Memory, 98
Mesland, Père, 23n
Moderation, 139–40
Monsters, 53, 56
Montaigne, Michel de, 161
Moore, C. A., 39n
Moral sense, 132
Morgan, Thomas, quoted, 84n
Mosley, Nicholas, 48n
Motion, necessity for life, 59, 133, 133n, 145, 150
Motivation, human: Tory and Whig positions on, 115, 124–25

Natural religion. See Religion, natural
Nature, 53, 71, 106–13, 137; as body of the world, 56; to be followed, 110–12, 142–43; personification of, 106–108; plastic, 8, 49–50, 71–73, 107n
Necessity, 23, 23n, 26–27, 30, 41, 61, 64; of the creation, 33–40, 68; logical, 30, 43; moral, 21, 30, 39, 169; in Pope's system, 33–35, 41, 68
Nero, 148, 159

Newton, Isaac, 27, 49, 73
Nichols, N., 116n
Norris, John, 89; quoted, 83n, 85n, 88n, 89

Obligation, moral, source of, 4–5, 21, 66, 101, 116–25
Optimism, 42
Order, 151, 171
Organic theory of human personality, 160
Origen, 46, 52

Pain. See Pleasure and pain
Papillon, David, 136n, 137n
Pascal, Blaise, 85n
Passion: predominant or ruling: 9, 62n, 106, 108, 134, 139–40, 144–72, 165n; danger of, 9, 145, 150; divine, 167–72; and the humors, 150–60; literary theories of, 160–61; and moral determinism, 152–54, 158; organic origin of, 146; philosophical bases for, 161–66; predominant virtue grafted to, 147
Passions: 87, 94; balance of, 136–37, 148–54; baseness of, 136; caprice of, 146; dangers of, 133, 134, 136; moderating or restraining of, 136–40, 146; as modes of self–love, 94, 176; moral neutrality of, 133, 134; necessity for, 133, 135; predominant in man, 12, 126, 135–36, 138–39, 144, 150; productive of good, 133, 134; subordination to reason, 111–12, 127–28; winds of, 140–42
Pattison, Mark, 181
Paxton, Peter, 159n
Pilot, reason as, 97, 141–42
Plato, 45
Platonists, 86
Pleasure and pain, 100–103, 108, 137, 172, 176

Pope, Alexander: antagonist of, 13–18, 68, 167; *The Dunciad*, 153; *Epilogue to the Satires*, 153; *Epistle "To Augustus,"* 153; *Epistle to Bathurst*, quoted, 165n; *Epistle to Cobham*, 145, 145n, 160; *Essay on Criticism*, 54, 76, 107n; *Essay on Man:* and Christianity, 11; commonplace ideas in, 4, 7, 9; danger of sacrilege in, 10; dualism of, 172; system of natural religion, 11–12; tone of, 9–10; wit of, 9–10, 191

Pride, 36, 87–88, 90, 98, 118, 127, 136, 148, 153, 174, 183

Providence, divine, 44, 72, 90. *See also* Immensity, God's attribute of

Puritans, 95

Qualities, moral, divine. *See* God, moral attributes of

Quality, in humors theory, 155, 155n

Range of ideas. *See* Spectrum of ideas

Rationalists, Anglican, 16n, 78, 95

Ray, John, 72

Reason: abstract, 137–39, 143; analogical, 77–82; divine, 21–22, 28; personified, 90–91; sufficient (Liebniz's principle of), 21, 28–29. *See also* Reason, human

Reason, human: as comparing power, 91–94; guides to, 100–115, 137; passivity of, 91, 93, 117; predominance over passions and self-love, 16n, 75–76, 94, 111–12, 115, 126–28, 133, 135–37, 144, 176–77, 184–85; restraining power of, 97, 108; as tool, 91, 128, 138–39, 141–43; weakness of, 77, 91, 126, 137; and what we know, 77, 82–85

Reason of things, 5, 20, 25–26, 37–38, 62, 66, 114–115, 119–22, 139, 169–70, 172. *See also* Things, differences of

Redwine, James D., 157n, 158n

Religion, natural: and deism, 11; *Essay on Man* as system of, 11, 125, 137; and revelation, 11–12, 16n; systems of, 11–12, 95

Revelation, and natural religion, 11–12, 16n, 95, 125

Rewards and punishments, 14–16, 16n, 123, 125, 177

Reynolds, Edward, 88n, 134n, 135n, 136n, 137n

Robinson, Nicholas, 160n

Robinson, Thomas, 48n

Ruling passion. *See* Passion, predominant

St. John, Henry. *See* Bolingbroke, Henry St. John

Salvation, 95, 117

Scale of Being. *See* Chain of being

Science, 88–90

Scott, John, 47

Scriblerus club, 138n

Selfishness, 96, 174, 186–87

Self-love, 62n, 66, 87, 90, 91, 94, 95–97, 102, 110, 113, 120–22, 137, 142, 166–67, 172; ambiguity of term, 174–75; cool, 185–86; enlightened, 96, 139, 142; neutrality of, 96, 177, 183–87; as one of the passions, 129–32; passions as modes of, 128, 176; predominant in man, 5, 8–9, 16n, 75–76, 96–97, 115, 125, 133, 137, 138, 153, 173–83; as self-preservation, 96, 134, 175, 184; and social the same, 9, 101, 125, 130, 177, 180, 182, 187–90

Senault, Jean-François, 136n, 137–38, 150–51, 153, 154; quoted, 138, 149

Seneca, 45, 50, 58; quoted, 58

Senses, as limits of knowledge, 80, 82, 86–87, 91–94
Shadwell, Thomas, 157–58n
Shaftesbury, Anthony Ashley Cooper, 3d Earl of, 101, 104n, 105, 110, 128, 132, 161n, 166, 189; quoted, 190n
Sherlock, William, 15
Ship, metaphor for the passions, 140–42
Snuggs, Henry L., 156n
Socinianism, 116
Soul: immortality of, 11, 12; philosophical and popular definitions of, 52, 53; rational, 54; sensitive, 54; vegetative, 8, 49, 55, 106
Soul of the world, God as, 8, 41–73
Spectator, The, 133–34, 137n, 140–41; quoted, 133–34, 140–41
Spectrum of ideas, defined, 1–6
Spence, Joseph, 10
Spinoza, Benedict, 20, 26–27
Spirit, Mosaical, 50, 54
Stackhouse, Thomas, quoted, 48
Stanley, Thomas, 46n
Status of ideas, defined, 6
Stevens, Nicholas, 15
Stoicism, 127–28, 133–34, 139, 161; fatalism of, 127; and suppression of the passions, 127–28
Swift, Jonathan, 10n, 14, 39n, 161n
Sykes, Arthur Ashley, 115–25, 166; quoted, 118, 119, 121, 125

Tave, Stuart M., 161n
Temperament, and humors psychology, 150–51
Tenison, Thomas, quoted, 184
Things, differences of, 64–67, 110–14. See also Reason of things

Tillotson, John, 12, 15–16, 32, 46, 135n; quoted, 15–16, 32, 46
Tindal, Matthew, 12, 16n; quoted, 190n
Titus, 148, 159
Toland, John, 92n

Underhill, Edward, 116n

Virgil, 45
Virtue, 101–103, 127–28, 136, 147; abstract ideas of, 128, 175; grafted to ruling passion, 147, 166; rigorous and consequential definitions of, 125, 166, 174, 177, 181–83, 189–91, 175n
Voltaire, 20, 42

War, Hobbes and the state of, 174
Warburton, William, 104, 141n, 181
Waterland, Daniel, 16n, 66, 115–25, 135, 166, 169; quoted, 116–17, 118, 119, 120, 122–23
Wesley, Samuel, 15
Wilkins, John, 32; quoted, 32, 184n
Will, arbitrary, 20, 23, 28
Will. See Free will
Willey, Basil, 109
Williams, Aubrey, 107n
Wisdom: infinite, and the best possible world, 7, 14, 19–40, 44, 169; as God's predominant attribute, 7, 8, 27–34, 145
Wollaston, William, 11, 104, 108n, 110–12, 135, 136n, 137n; quoted, 84n, 85n, 105, 110, 111–12
World: best possible, 17, 19–40, 42, 44, 64; as organism rather than mechanism, 42, 45. See also Soul of the world
Wright, Thomas, 136n, 174–75n